MICROWAVE COOKING TIMES

D0618975

MICROWAVE COOKING TIMES

Jan Orchard

Edited/Updated by Carolyn Humphries

W. Foulsham & Co. Ltd.
London • New York • Toronto • Cape Town • Sydney

W. Foulsham & Company Limited
The Publishing House, Bennetts Close, Cippenham,
Berkshire, SL1 5AP

ISBN 0-572-01400-7

Copyright © 1994 W. Foulsham & Co. Ltd.

Printed in Great Britain by St Edmundsbury Press Ltd.,
Bury St Edmunds.

CONTENTS

GOLDEN RULES FOR MICROWAVE SUCCESS

As a microwave owner, you'll know the basics of how your machine
works. But do you know how to select, prepare and time foods to make
the best of this cooking method? Used well, a microwave is the best friend
any cook can have. Used badly, the microwave is a disappointing piece of
equipment. In each chapter of this book, we'll tell you how to prepare and
time foods to give successful results every time. But, before you begin,
follow these golden rules. Always follow the manufacturer's instructions.

FOOD TEMPERATURE

Food which is taken straight from the refrigerator will take longer to
re-heat or cook than food at room temperature. Some foods – like
vegetables – can be cooked straight from the freezer. These will,
obviously, take longer than defrosted or fresh ones.

WHAT SORT OF FOOD?

In general, the most successful foods to cook in a microwave are those
that are normally cooked by moist cooking methods such as steaming,
stewing, poaching or braising.

● Vegetables, fish, sauces, egg dishes (not boiled eggs), steamed
sponge mixture, custards and fruit. (Vegetables, fruit and fish are
particularly good, as flavour and colour are retained.)

● Chicken and turkey will be moist and delicious. They can be
browned in a roasting bag, then the skin crisped under the grill.

● Bacon, gammon, game and casseroles are good.

● Don't use your microwave for plain chops, steaks or cutlets, unless
you have a really good browning dish or a dual microwave/grill.

● For best results don't use it for the complete cooking of roasts of red
meat or pork. These meats can be started in the microwave and
completed in the main oven if you are in a hurry.

THE RIGHT SORT OF DISH

Not all cookware and crockery is suitable for microwaving. Generally those that are dishwasherproof will be fine in the microwave. Don't use plastic containers for foods that contain a lot of sugar and fat – ovenproof glass is better.

YOU CAN USE:
● Ovenproof glass, specially made microwave ware, glazed earthenware, dishwasher-safe porcelain, pottery, boilable plastic and wood.

YOU CAN'T USE:
● Metal, thin plastics, ironstone, or any crockery with metal decoration.

THE SAFE DISH TEST
If you're unsure if a dish is suitable, place it in the microwave with a glass half-full of water. Microwave on FULL/HIGH for 1 minute. The water should be warm, the dish cool. If it feels hot, it is made from materials which absorb microwaves and should not be used.

Size and shape are all important:
● Choose round or oblong dishes with straight sides, rather than square ones with corners.

● When cooking vegetables etc, the dish should be large enough to have food in a single layer.

● For casseroles and other food in liquid, the dish should be deep enough to take 5cm (2in) food with a space above to allow for boiling.

● For cakes and bread, there must be enough height for rising.

PREPARING THE FOOD

Microwaves penetrate food to a depth of about 5cm (2in). After that, cooking is by heat conduction which becomes gradually weaker towards the centre of a thick piece of food, so size and shape of food is important.

● Several small, even-sized pieces of food will cook more efficiently than a large piece of the same thing.

● When cooking a casserole or vegetables, make sure the pieces of food are all more or less the same size. If this is impossible, place the smaller pieces towards the middle of the dish.

● If possible, have an empty space at the centre of the dish. This gives a bigger area of exposure to microwaves. (Microwave-safe ring moulds are very useful.)

- When cooking fillets of meat or fish, turn the thickest part towards the microwave walls and protect the thin end, with a small, smooth, piece of foil. The foil should not touch the side of the oven.

- Protruding bone ends, such as chicken or turkey legs, should also be protected with foil.

- Foods cooked in individual dishes should be arranged in a circle, as should jacket potatoes, baked apples and other larger pieces of fruit or vegetables.

- Small pieces of food, and food in liquid, should be arranged in an even layer. A depth of around 5–7.5cm (2–3in) is ideal.

BROWNING THE FOOD

Many people are put off microwaving foods because they don't brown. But there are several ways of overcoming this:

For savoury foods either:
- Before cooking brush meat or poultry with melted butter or oil and dust with paprika OR equal quantities of water and mushroom or tomato ketchup, Worcestershire, soy or brown sauce.

- Brush with a glaze – marmalade, redcurrant jelly or honey are good – half way through cooking.

- Use a grill or frying pan to sear and brown surfaces before cooking in the microwave.

- Brown toppings or crisp skin under the grill at end of cooking.

- Use a browning dish for chops, steak etc (see p.22).

For cakes and bread:
- Scatter cinnamon, chopped nuts, desiccated coconut or chopped glacé fruits over surface of cakes before cooking OR sprinkle with a mixture of light brown sugar and chopped toasted nuts half way through.

- Dust with caster or icing sugar or decorate with butter cream or melted chocolate.

- Use brown instead of white sugar in the mixture (cakes flavoured with chocolate or coffee look fine).

- Use wholemeal instead of white flour – but you may need a little extra liquid.

- Brush bread and rolls with egg yolk and dust with cracked wheat, sesame or poppy seeds before cooking.

- Crisp and brown bread crust under a hot grill after cooking.

COVERING FOOD

A cover helps to retain moisture and speeds up the cooking process. As a general rule, always cover food to be microwaved unless the recipe states otherwise. The type of covering depends on the food being cooked. For safety, remove food wrap carefully after cooking.

• Use a microwave-safe dish with matching lid for vegetables, fruit, pasta, rice, casseroles, fish and sauces. Or use clingfilm. Stretch the film over the top of the dish and pierce it once. This prevents a rush of trapped steam when you uncover the dish after cooking. **If you are worried by recent reports on the possible dangers of using clingfilm, use a PVC-free type such as Purecling**.

• Use absorbent kitchen paper to cover dishes which give out moisture during re-heating, like bread, cakes and pastry. Do not use recycled paper. It can also be used to cover bacon rashers, but tends to stick. A microwave roasting dish with a grid and a dome cover is better.

• Never use large pieces of foil for covering food during cooking. The microwaves will bounce off the surface, called arcing, which can damage the oven. It is safe to use small pieces to protect bones etc.

FINDING THE RIGHT SETTING

Although most foods are cooked on FULL/HIGH the other settings on your microwave can be used. Casseroles have more flavour and a better texture if started on FULL/HIGH then reduced to DEFROST/MED-LOW. Sensitive foods, such as cheese, eggs, cream, mushrooms and shellfish are better cooked on SIMMER/MEDIUM. The chart on page 15 explains the different settings used by manufacturers.

STIRRING AND STANDING

Because the outer edges cook first in the microwave, whenever possible, food should be stirred or gently re-arranged at least once during cooking.

• Stir from the outside of the dish, so that the centre portions are brought to the edge.

- Large pieces of food (such as a chicken) should be turned over once during cooking.
- If you have a microwave without a turntable, turn the dish round at least once during cooking.
- Food continues to cook after it has been removed from the microwave. This is a result of heat conduction, not from lingering microwaves. With larger quantities of food, standing time is essential to complete cooking. Always follow timings given in the recipe or chart, and wrap or cover food with foil, shiny side in, to retain the heat.
- Standing time is vital for even defrosting. Long exposure to microwaves, even on DEFROST/MED-LOW setting, means food will begin to cook at the edges. Standing time allows the heat to spread from edge to centre, giving even defrosting.

TIMING

- The charts in this book are designed to give a guide to times for many different types of food cooked or defrosted in 500, 600/650, 700, and 800/850w microwave ovens.
- The size and shape of food, its density, the amount of fat and sugar, the shape of the dish and the way the microwave performs all affect cooking and defrosting times.
- Remember, the more you cook, the longer it takes. In a conventional oven, one baked potato takes the same time as four baked potatoes. In a microwave, four potatoes take much longer to cook than just one.
- Food cooked in a microwave doesn't burn, but it does turn rock hard if overcooked. It is well worth testing foods half a minute or so before the end of cooking time; microwaving is not an exact science, as all ovens perform slightly differently. So get to know yours and use the blank pages at the back of this book to jot down useful information.

DEFROSTING

Quick defrosting is one of the great benefits of owning a microwave oven. Most models have a defrost setting, and many have automatic defrosting where microwave energy is pulsed on and off, so that standing time is built in.

The setting for defrosting is usually 30 percent of full power.

The rules relating to the size, shape and arrangement which are given for cooking food also apply to food to be defrosted. In addition, remember the following:

• When defrosting food which will give out a lot of liquid, stand the food on a rack so that the liquid drips away. If food stands in the liquid, it will also cook as a result of the liquid being heated from the action of microwaves.

• Check food before the end of the given defrosting time. Remember that standing time will thaw ice left at the centre.

• Remove lids, open containers, and slit plastic pouches before defrosting food in a liquid. Liquid may expand as it defrosts and will force lids and covers off.

• If possible, separate food to be defrosted into pieces. Arrange in the same way as food to be cooked.

• When defrosting minced meat, a casserole or other food in a block, break down the edges as they thaw and move the frozen part to the edge. Mince should be scraped away and removed from the oven as it thaws. Free-flow mince can be cooked from frozen.

• If the food is in a bag, flex the bag gently from time to time as it thaws to distribute heat.

• Don't try to defrost poultry completely in a microwave oven. Start defrosting of whole birds in the microwave, then complete thawing at room temperature. Salmonella, an organism which causes a particularly nasty form of food poisoning, can flourish in poultry which is cooked before it has thawed all the way through. It is, however, safe to defrost poultry portions in the microwave. Clean the oven after use to avoid possible contamination.

• When defrosting cakes, bread and other bakes, place them on and cover with a sheet of absorbent kitchen paper to soak up moisture.

• Make sure twist ties on food bags don't have a metal centre.

• Wrap food in foil, shiny side in, during standing time. This encourages uniform thawing.

• Vegetables can be cooked straight from frozen.

• Protect thin edges of food with smooth pieces of foil as they thaw. This is particularly important with meat and fish, which may start to cook during thawing.

• Never try to defrost any food completely in the microwave. The edges will cook and harden before this happens. Remember that defrosting continues during standing time.

USING THE CHARTS

When using the cooking charts, check food at the shortest cooking time given, then after every 30 seconds. Microwave timings depend on the type of oven you are using, the shape of the dish and the arrangement of food being cooked, so 'exact-to-the-second' timings are impossible.

MICROWAVE POWER GUIDE

As there's no standard power indicator on microwave ovens, our chart will help you to find the right setting.

Nos	1	2	3	4	5
Description	Warm Low	Defrost Med-Low	Simmer Medium	Roast Medium/ High	Full High
Percentage	10	30	50	70	100

MEAT

Not all meat dishes work well in a microwave, so, it is best to be selective and avoid disappointment.

MINCED MEAT

Minced meat cooks well in a microwave, either with or without a sauce. There is no need to add fat. Simply spread the meat in a thin layer in a shallow dish cover and cook on FULL/HIGH, following times given in the chart (page 41). Pour the melted fat from the dish before adding sauce or vegetables.

CHOPS AND STEAKS

• Chops and steaks cook well in the microwave if a browning dish is used. A browning dish is a special microwave product, the base of which is coated with a layer of heat-retaining material. The dish is first pre-heated in the microwave. When food is placed on the base of the hot dish, the surface is seared, and browned. The browning dish chart (page 22) gives time for chops, steaks, sausages, beefburgers and other meats suited to this cooking method.

• They can also be cooked in a sauce in a casserole dish. Choose chops or steaks of equal size if you want to cook more than one at a time. Cook with the thickest edge of meat to the outside of the dish.

OFFAL

Liver and kidneys cook quickly and well in a microwave – especially in a sauce. Make sure they are cut to even sized pieces and take care not to overcook as the flesh toughens easily.

Hearts need long, slow cooking and are best cooked one day then re-heated the next.

CASSEROLES

● For tender, tasty results, microwaved casseroles must be cooked on DEFROST/MED-LOW for almost as long as in a conventional oven. The advantage lies in fuel saving, since casseroling in a microwave uses much less energy than a conventional gas or electric oven.

● The average cooking time for a microwave casserole is 90 minutes. Most casseroles taste better if cooked the day before and just re-heated before eating.

● Add less liquid when cooking a microwave casserole – it won't cook down as much as meat cooked in a conventional oven.

● To adapt conventional recipes, reduce the liquid by about half.

● Sensitive vegetables, such as mushrooms, should be added towards the end of the cooking time.

● Meat and vegetables for casseroling should be cut into pieces of roughly the same size.

● Season the casserole after cooking, not before. Remember that microwaving preserves flavour so if you have used stock cubes, extra seasoning may not be necessary.

BACON AND GAMMON

Bacon rashers cook well in the microwave because the high percentage of fat to lean encourages browning.

● Always cook rashers on a grid with a dish beneath to catch fat drips.

● Cover the bacon with a dome, an upturned bowl or with absorbent kitchen paper (although kitchen paper tends to stick) to prevent splashes of fat.

● Cook on FULL/HIGH for 30–60 seconds per rasher.

   Gammon rashers and bacon chops can be cooked on a rack or on a browning dish. Always remove the rind from bacon and gammon and snip fat at intervals to stop the meat curling as it cooks.
   Stuffed bacon rolls (Angels on Horseback) can be microwaved.

Make the rolls in the usual way and secure them with wooden cocktail sticks.

Gammon and bacon joints keep their shape and flavour when cooked in the microwave and are especially good if you want to slice the meat and serve it cold. Unless the joint is one of the pre-shaped, round kinds, it must be soaked overnight in two or three changes of water. Otherwise salt will remain in the meat rather than dissolving as it does when boiled or cooked in a conventional oven and the result will be unbearably salty.

• Always cook gammon and bacon joints in a roasting bag. If you want to glaze the fat, remove the rind after cooking, cut the surface of the fat into diamond shapes, brush with warmed honey or marmalade and brown under a conventional grill.

PATES AND TERRINES

Pâtés and terrines take up to 3 hours in a conventional oven but a typical pâté containing 900g (2lb) of meat can be cooked in about 20 minutes in the microwave. As with conventionally cooked pâtés, the end result should be weighted and left overnight.

ROASTING JOINTS

Small pieces of meat such as stuffed pork or lamb tenderloin, work well. And although it is possible to cook a joint of meat in a microwave (and many oven manufacturers and recipe books will tell you how), the results are not appealing. Larger joints will brown slightly if cooked in a roasting bag, but the fat won't be crisp. The meat itself will look grey and taste steamed. A conventional oven makes a far better job of traditional beef, pork, lamb and veal roasts. However, we have included a roasting chart for those who may wish to use it.

• If time is short, compromise. Start roasting joint in the microwave and finish it in the conventional oven. This works best with lamb and pork. Allow 7–9 minutes per 450g (1lb) of meat on FULL/HIGH, and give 450–900g (1–2lb) of cooking time, depending on the size of the joint, then cook the remaining 'pounds' in the conventional oven for the usual time. If, for instance, you wanted to speed the cooking of a 2.5kg (5lb) leg of lamb, cook it in the microwave in a roasting bag for 14 minutes then in the conventional oven for 1 hour (20 minutes per 450g/1lb). This reduces the cooking time to 1 hour 14 minutes instead of

2 hours. If the joint was cooked completely in the microwave, the time would be 1 hour 5 minutes (including standing time), which is not very much quicker, so for the sake of 9 minutes it is worth taking the microwave/conventional option for a better tasting piece of meat.

GOLDEN RULES FOR MEAT COOKERY

● Always position meat with the thickest part towards the outside. Protect thin parts and bone ends with small, smooth pieces of foil.

● Meat must be completely thawed before microwaving. See defrost charts (pages 32–33).

● If using a browning dish for more than one batch of food, remember that it will need re-heating before the second batch of food is added.

● If meat is skewered, the skewers must be made of wood.

● Make sure roasting bag ties are all plastic, not metal with a plastic covering.

● Don't use a conventional meat thermometer in a microwave (but it can be used after meat has been removed from oven). Special microwave thermometers are available and some ovens have a built-in probe.

● Don't salt meat before cooking.

● When using a roasting bag, put the meat on a rack with a small slit in the bag at the bottom or sides. This allows liquid to drain away.

BARBECUES

● Chicken, chops and sausages can be cooked first in the microwave then finished off on the barbecue so that the authentic smoky flavour is imparted to the food.

MEAT THERMOMETER CHART

The joint should feel tender when tested with a skewer, when cooked. But for best results use a microwave thermometer or probe.

'Remember, the temperature inside the joint will rise by 50°F/10°C during standing time, so allow for this when checking for doneness.

BEEF

BONED AND ROLLED

HOW COOKED	Rare	Medium	Well done
THERMOMETER, TEMP. WHEN COOKED, AFTER STANDING TIME			
	140°F (60°C)	160°F (70°C)	175°F (80°C)

LAMB

LEG OR SHOULDER

HOW COOKED	Medium	Well done
THERMOMETER TEMP. WHEN COOKED, AFTER STANDING TIME		
	160°F (70°C)	175°F (80°C)

PORK

LEG, LOIN OR HAND

HOW COOKED	Well done
THERMOMETER TEMP. WHEN COOKED, AFTER STANDING TIME	
	175°F (80°C)

VEAL

HOW COOKED Well done

THERMOMETER TEMP. WHEN COOKED, AFTER STANDING TIME

175°F
(80°C)

BROWNING DISH TIMES

A browning dish can be used to sear and brown the surface of many foods.

1. Pre-heat dish on FULL/HIGH for 8 minutes (500w), 6–7 minutes (600/650w), 5–6 minutes (700w) and 4–5 minutes 800/850w).

2. Add a knob of butter or 1 tbsp oil, swirl round dish.

3. Press the food to be cooked, thinest parts to the middle, on the dish. Cook on FULL/HIGH for times listed below. Turn food over as stated.

4. Shield any thin parts with foil if overcooking.

5. If cooking a second batch of food, re-heat the dish for half the original heating time.

NOTE: Always use oven gloves to hold dish and allow to cool before submerging in water. Check manufacturer's instructions before use.

STEAK

QUANTITY	COOKING TIME IN MINUTES			
	500w	600/650w	700w	800/850w
200–225g (8oz)	3½–5	3–4	2½–3½	2–3

WATCHPOINTS

Turn steak over half way through cooking.

CHOPS

QUANTITY	COOKING TIME IN MINUTES			
	500w	600/650w	700w	800/850w
2 large or 4 cutlets	7	6	5	4

WATCHPOINTS

Turn over once half way through cooking.

GAMMON/HAM STEAKS

QUANTITY	COOKING TIME IN MINUTES			
	500w	*600/650w*	*700w*	*800/850w*
2 medium	5–6	4–5	3½–4	3–3½

PREPARATION

Snip edge of fat with scissors to prevent curling.

WATCHPOINTS

Turn over once half way through cooking.

HAMBURGERS

QUANTITY	COOKING TIME IN MINUTES			
	500w	*600/650w*	*700w*	*800/850w*
2 (quarterpounders) or 4 small	3½	3	2½	2

WATCHPOINTS

Don't add extra fat. Turn over once half way through cooking.

SAUSAGES

QUANTITY	COOKING TIME IN MINUTES			
	500w	*600/650w*	*700w*	*800/850w*
8 chipolatas	3½–5	3–4	2½–3½	2–2½
8 large	7	6	5	4

PREPARATION

prick before cooking.

WATCHPOINTS

Don't add extra fat. Turn several times during cooking.

'TOASTED' SANDWICHES

QUANTITY	COOKING TIME IN MINUTES			
	500w	*600/650w*	*700w*	*800/850w*
2 rounds	3½	3	2½	2

PREPARATION

Butter bread on outside of sandwiches.

FISH FINGERS

QUANTITY	COOKING TIME IN MINUTES			
	500w	*600/650w*	*700w*	*800/850w*
4	3½	3	2½	2

WATCHPOINTS

Cook from frozen. Turn over once half way through cooking.

FISH CAKES

QUANTITY	COOKING TIME IN MINUTES			
	500w	*600/650w*	*700w*	*800/850w*
4	7	6	5	4

WATCHPOINTS

Cook from frozen. Turn over once half way through cooking.

POTATO WAFFLES

QUANTITY	COOKING TIME IN MINUTES			
	500w	*600/650w*	*700w*	*800/850w*
2	5	4	3½	3

WATCHPOINTS

Cook from frozen. Turn over once half way through cooking.

PIZZA

QUANTITY	COOKING TIME IN MINUTES			
	500w	*600/650w*	*700w*	*800/850w*
18cm (7in) round	7	6	5	4

WATCHPOINTS

Cook from frozen. Do not turn over. Cooking time depends on thickness so keep checking for doneness.

MEAT ROASTING TIMES

Microwaving is not the ideal way to cook a joint. It is better to start the joint in the microwave and finish it in the conventional oven, as explained in the section on roast meat (page 18). But if you do want to use your microwave totally, here are the cooking times. Always use a roasting bag. This prevents splashing and encourages the meat to brown. Put the bag on a roasting rack with a slit in the plastic at the bottom or side. This allows liquid to drain away. Stand the rack on a microwave-proof plate or tray to catch the drips.

Cook on FULL/HIGH and turn halfway through cooking. Stand wrapped in foil, shiny side in. Use a meat thermometer during standing time to check the internal temperature of the joint. (See chart on page 20.)

NOTE

● To cook on ROAST/MED-HIGH add 2 minutes per 450g (1lb) to the cooking time.

● These times are at room temperature. If cooking straight from the refrigerator add another 1–2 minutes per 450g (1lb).

BEEF

BONED SIRLOIN OR TOPSIDE

PREPARATION

Put in a roasting bag on a rack, fat side down.

COOKING TIME IN MINUTES PER 450g (1lb)

	500w	600/650w	700w	800/850w
Rare	6–7	5–6	4–5	3½–4
Medium	8½–9½	7–8	6–7	5–5½
Well done	11–12	9–10	7½–8½	6½–7

STANDING TIME

15–20 minutes for rare, 20–25 minutes for medium/well done

WATCHPOINTS

Check condition of joint by inserting a meat thermometer at thickest part during standing. (See Meat Thermometer Chart on page 20 for temperature at which joint will be cooked.)

ON BONE (RIB)

PREPARATION

Put joint in a roasting bag and place on a rack. Protect bone ends with small smooth pieces of foil.

COOKING TIME IN MINUTES PER 450g (1lb)

	500w	*600/650w*	*700w*	*800/850w*
Rare	5–6	4–5	3½–4	3–3½
Medium	7–8	6–7	5–6	4–5
Well done	9½–11	8–9	7–8	5½–6

STANDING TIME

As above

VEAL

BONED, ROLLED (LEG/SHOULDER)

PREPARATION

Put in a roasting bag on a rack, fat side down.

COOKING TIME IN MINUTES PER 450g (1lb)

500w	*600/650w*	*700w*	*800/850w*
11–12	9–10	7½–8½	6½–7

STANDING TIME

25–30 minutes

WATCHPOINTS

Remember to turn halfway through.

ON BONE (LEG/SHOULDER)

PREPARATION

Protect bone end with foil. Put in a bag, fat side down.

COOKING TIME IN MINUTES PER 450g (1lb)

500w	*600/650w*	*700w*	*800/850w*
9½–11	8–9	7–8	5½–6

STANDING TIME

30 minutes wrapped in foil

WATCHPOINTS

As above

PORK

BONED, ROLLED

PREPARATION

Place in a roasting bag on a rack, fat side down.

COOKING TIME IN MINUTES PER 450g (1lb)

500w	600/650w	700w	800/850w
11–12	9–10	7½–8½	6½–7

STANDING TIME

30 minutes wrapped in foil

WATCHPOINTS

For crisp crackling, cut fat away at start of standing time. Score fat.
Put on a roasting rack. Cover and cook on FULL/HIGH checking
every minute until the fat is crisp.

LAMB

LEG, SHOULDER

PREPARATION

Place in roasting bag on a rack. Cover bone end with foil.

COOKING TIME IN MINUTES PER 450g (1lb) as for *VEAL ON BONE*

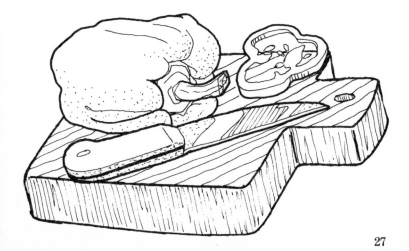

DEFROSTING MEAT

With a microwave, joints can be thawed in under 2 hours, and most smaller cuts in under an hour. But it isn't simply a matter of putting the meat in and turning the microwave to DEFROST. Meat needs careful treatment, otherwise the edges will begin to cook before the centre has thawed.

● Chops, steaks, sausages, offal, bacon, mince and meat for casseroling can be thawed successfully see chart p.35.

● Joints are best started in the microwave then left to complete thawing at room temperature. Most joints are an uneven shape, and this makes uniform thawing difficult. Our chart on p.32 shows how to start thawing a joint in the microwave and complete the process in under 2 hours.

● Small, thin pieces of meat can be thawed and cooked in one operation, but results are not very good (with the exception of beefburgers) so when possible, thaw then cook.

PREPARING FOR DEFROSTING

Meat gives out liquid during defrosting, so a rack is essential. Choose a rack which fits inside a shallow dish. This allows liquid to drip through. If you allow the meat to stand in the liquid, it will begin to cook as the liquid heats up.

JOINTS

● Start joint in freezer wrapper. After 15 minutes, unwrap.

● If it has a bone, protect the ends with small, smooth pieces of foil.

● Stand the joint on the rack and cover with clingfilm or plastic dome.

● If the joint is an uneven shape (such as a leg or shoulder), position with the thickest part towards the outside. If the joint is big and it isn't possible to do this, protect the thinnest end with a smooth piece of foil.

MEAT IN SLICES

Thick slices of meat (such as braising steak) often stick together when frozen.

- Start the meat thawing in its pack.

- As soon as it has defrosted sufficiently, separate the pieces and arrange them on the rack so that the thickest edges are towards the outside.

- Cover with clingfilm or a dome and continue defrosting.

MEAT IN CUBES

- If the meat has been free flow frozen (i.e. isn't stuck together), arrange the cubes on the rack and cover. As the meat thaws, move the frozen pieces from the centre to the edge.

- If the meat has been frozen in a solid block, put it on the rack, cover and remove cubes as they thaw. Wrap the part-thawed cubes in foil.

SAUSAGES

- If the sausages are stuck together, start thawing them in their pack, then free them as soon as possible.

- Arrange around the edge of the rack to finish defrosting.

- Free flow sausages should be arranged in a circle around the edge of the rack. Make an inner circle and change the sausages around as they begin to thaw.

BACON RASHERS

- Start bacon rashers thawing in their pack. As soon as the top rasher is soft, open the pack and peel away as many rashers as you can.

- Continue thawing on the rack, peeling rashers away as soon as they become soft enough.

MINCED MEAT

- If the meat is free flow frozen, there is no need to thaw it before cooking.

- Mince frozen in a block should be put on the rack then covered with clingfilm or a dome. As the edges begin to thaw scrape the meat away and set aside in a foil-covered bowl.

- Break up the block as soon as possible. If this is not done, the outside will cook while the centre remains frozen.

- Sausagemeat should be thawed in the same way.

COOKED MEAT DISHES

- Frozen, cooked meat dishes containing a sauce (i.e. casseroles, spaghetti bolognaise, etc) can be thawed and re-heated in one operation.

- If the casserole was frozen in a microwave-safe dish, it can be thawed/re-heated in the same dish. If it wasn't you will have to transfer the meat to a suitable container.

- As the casserole or meat dish begins to thaw, the edges will melt. Break up the block as this happens and stir, so that the colder parts are pushed to the outer edges.

- Casseroles and other meat dishes containing a sauce should be thawed/re-heated on FULL/HIGH not on DEFROST/MED-LOW.

- Don't try this with meat pies (the pastry turns soggy), pâtés (the fat begins to melt) or slices of meat (they dry out).

STANDING TIMES

- Standing time is important for good results. During standing time, heat spreads through the food, thawing the centre where microwaves cannot penetrate. Unless otherwise stated, always wrap food in foil, shiny side in, during standing time. This keeps the heat in and encourages thawing.

- If you have a microwave with automatic or cyclic defrosting, it will pulse energy on and off during the selected thawing time, so that standing time is built into the process. It is still a good idea to give some foil-wrapped standing time at the end of defrosting for even results.

NOTE: Extra microwaving will not cut the standing time, so don't be tempted. All that will happen is that the outside of the meat will begin to cook while the centre remains frozen.

DEFROST SETTINGS

Most microwaves have a DEFROST/MED-LOW setting. This is usually 30 percent of the total power. There is no need to use different times for different machines at this power level.

NOTE: Some lower-wattage machines defrost at 50 percent power. Check your manufacturer's instructions if in doubt.

JOINT THAWING TIMES

Complete thawing of a joint in the microwave is almost impossible without cooking the edges. Our method reduces the time needed for natural thawing, after microwaving and standing, to about 1 hour, depending on the size of the joint.

• If you do need to thaw a joint completely in the microwave for immediate cooking, prepare as below but thaw on WARM/LOW (10 percent power) for 21–23 minutes per 450g (1lb).

BEEF

ON BONE

DEFROST TIME PER 450g (1lb)

5–8 minutes

STANDING TIME

Wrap in foil and stand for 30 minutes halfway through. At end, complete thawing naturally.

WATCHPOINTS

Protect bone with foil. If edges begin to cook cover with foil. Turn joint over half-way through cooking.

ROLLED

DEFROST TIME PER 450g (1lb)

10 minutes

STANDING TIME

As above

WATCHPOINTS

As above

LAMB

ON BONE

DEFROST TIME PER 450g (1lb)

6 minutes

STANDING TIME

As for Beef

WATCHPOINTS

As for Beef

OFF BONE

DEFROST TIME PER 450g (1lb)

8 minutes

STANDING TIME

As for Beef

WATCHPOINTS

As for Beef

PORK

ON BONE

DEFROST TIME PER 450g (1lb)

8 minutes

STANDING TIME

As for Beef

WATCHPOINTS

As for Beef

OFF BONE

DEFROST TIME PER 450g (1lb)

10 minutes

STANDING TIME

As for Beef

WATCHPOINTS

As for Beef

HAM

ON BONE

DEFROST TIME PER 450g (1lb)

8 minutes

STANDING TIME

As for Beef

WATCHPOINTS

As for Beef

OFF BONE

DEFROST TIME PER 450g (1lb)

10 minutes

STANDING TIME AND WATCHPOINTS

As for Beef

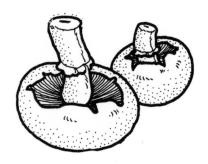

SMALLER CUT THAWING TIMES

All times given are for DEFROST/MED-LOW/30 percent power.

STEAKS

DEFROST TIME PER 450g (1lb)

6–8 minutes

STANDING TIME

Wrap in foil. Stand 5–10 minutes

WATCHPOINTS

Protect thin edges with foil. Keep thickest part to outside during thawing. If stuck together, separate as soon as possible.

STEWING MEAT

IN SLICES

DEFROST TIME PER 450g (1lb)

8 minutes

STANDING TIME

Wrap in foil. Stand 10–12 minutes

WATCHPOINTS

As for Steaks.

IN CUBES

DEFROST TIMES PER 450g (1lb)

8 minutes

Wrap in foil. Stand 10–12 minutes

WATCHPOINTS

Separate meat as it defrosts if frozen in a block. Put part-thawed pieces in a bowl and cover with foil.

MINCED MEAT

DEFROST TIME PER 450g (1lb)

8 minutes

STANDING TIME

Put scraped-off thawed meat in foil-covered bowl.

WATCHPOINTS

Scrape thawed meat away and break up block as soon as possible

---

LAMB CHOPS

DEFROST TIME

5 minutes for 2
8 minutes for 4

STANDING TIME

Wrap in foil. Stand 5 minutes

WATCHPOINTS

Protect bone ends with foil. Place thickest edge towards outside when thawing. Four chops is maximum for one thaw.

PORK CHOPS

DEFROST TIME

8 minutes for 2
12 minutes for 4

STANDING TIME

Wrap in foil. Stand 5 minutes

WATCHPOINTS

If the chops have kidney, protect it with foil. Protect bone ends with foil. Four chops is maximum for one thaw.

LIVER

DEFROST TIME PER 450g (1lb)

8 minutes

STANDING TIME

Wrap in foil. Stand 5 minutes

WATCHPOINTS

Separate slices as liver thaws. Keep thick edges towards outside.

KIDNEYS

DEFROST TIME PER 450g (1lb)

8 minutes

STANDING TIME

Wrap in foil. Stand 5 minutes

WATCHPOINTS

If stuck together, separate pieces as kidneys thaw.

BACON RASHERS

DEFROST TIME PER 450g (1lb)

6 minutes

STANDING TIME

None

WATCHPOINTS

Separate rashers as they thaw.

SAUSAGES

DEFROST TIME PER 450g (1lb)

8 minutes

STANDING TIME

Wrap in foil. Stand 5 minutes

WATCHPOINTS

If stuck together, separate as they thaw.

SAUSAGEMEAT

AS FOR MINCED MEAT

COOKED MEAT DISHES

You can thaw and reheat many cooked meat dishes in one process. Always ensure food is piping hot before serving. The base of the dish should feel very hot and the blade of a knife plunged down through the centre and held for 5 seconds should come out feeling boiling hot.

- If reheating, *not* thawing, follow 'cooking times in minutes' and ignore defrost times.

NOTE: Time will depend on depth of food. Always check and add a little more time if necessary.

CASSEROLE

QUANTITY	COOKING TIME IN MINUTES ON FULL			
	500w	*600/650w*	*700w*	*800/850w*
2 portions (225g/ 8oz meat)	11–12	9–10	7½–8½	6½–7
4 portions (450g/ 1lb meat)	18–20	15–17	13–15	10½–12

STANDING TIME

Stand covered in foil for 2 minutes.

WATCHPOINTS

Stir as casserole thaws. Check seasoning before serving.

SHEPHERD'S PIE

QUANTITY

4 portions

COOKING AND STANDING TIME

Start on DEFROST for 6 minutes, then stand wrapped in foil for 6 minutes. Cook on FULL for 7 minutes (*500w*), 6 minutes (*600/650w*), 5 minutes (*700w*), 4 minutes (*800/850w*). Stand 6 minutes.

WATCHPOINTS

Return pie to microwave for 2–3 minutes after standing.

LASAGNE/MOUSSAKA

QUANTITY

4 portions

COOKING AND STANDING TIME

Start on DEFROST for 8 minutes. Stand for 6 minutes wrapped in foil.
Cook on FULL for 12 minutes (*500w*), 10 minutes (*600/650w*),
8½ minutes (*700w*), 7 minutes (*800/850w*). Stand 5 minutes.

WATCHPOINTS

As for Shepherd's Pie

ROAST MEAT FROZEN IN GRAVY

QUANTITY

100g (4oz)
225g (8oz)

COOKING AND STANDING TIME

Start on DEFROST for 5 minutes, then stand in foil for 4 minutes for
100g (4oz); 8 minutes for 225g (8oz). Cook on FULL/HIGH for 2
minutes (*500w*), 1½ minutes (*600/650w*), 1¼ minutes (*700w*), 1 minute
(*800/850w*) for 100g (4oz); 3½ minutes (*500w*), 3 minutes (*600/650w*), 2½
minutes, (*700w*), 2 minutes (*800/850w*) for 225g (8oz).

WATCHPOINTS

Separate slices after they defrost.

MINCED MEAT AND CASSEROLES COOKING TIMES

All times given are for cooking on DEFROST/MED-LOW (30 percent power). Times are the same for all ovens.

MINCE

PORK, LAMB OR BEEF

QUANTITY	COOKING TIME
225g (8oz)	5–10 minutes, then 25 minutes with sauce. For
450g (1lb)	plain mince, cook for 5–8 minutes on FULL/ HIGH depending on the amount.

PREPARATION

Break up and place in a thin layer in a shallow dish. If cooking with onion, sauté it first and add halfway through mince cooking time. Cover with pierced clingfilm. Add sauce after cooking.

STANDING TIME

5–10 minutes

WATCHPOINTS

Tent a piece of foil over the dish while standing. Test before end of cooking time.

CASSEROLE OF BEEF OR LAMB

CHUCK, STEWING, SKIRT, BRAISING, NECK, SHOULDER

QUANTITY	COOKING TIME
225g (8oz)	55–65 minutes
450g (1lb)	90–100 minutes

PREPARATION

Seal meat first on conventional heat. Sauté onion in microwave. Meat should be in even-sized pieces. Put in a wide, shallow dish with vegetables (also cut to a similar size) onion and stock. Use 150ml (¼pt)/ 300ml (½pt) hot stock. Cover with pierced clingfilm.

STANDING TIME

5–10 minutes

WATCHPOINTS

As for Mince, but leave overnight if possible and skim fat away when cold.

PORK

SPARE RIB, SHOULDER

QUANTITY	COOKING TIME
225g (8oz)	55–65 minutes
450g (1lb)	90–100 minutes

PREPARATION

Cut into even-sized pieces. Prepare as for beef casserole.

STANDING TIME

5–10 minutes

WATCHPOINTS

As for Mince. Skim off any surface fat.

VEGETABLES

Fresh and frozen vegetables are perfect for microwaving. Colour and flavour are preserved and the vegetables are tender but still slightly crisp, giving an interesting texture.

Vegetables can be cooked ahead of time, arranged in serving dishes then quickly re-heated in the microwave when needed without loss of flavour, colour or texture.

Frozen vegetables don't need thawing before cooking. If the vegetables are in a bag, there isn't any need to remove the packing. Just slit the bag and microwave for the time recommended in the chart.

Pulses, such as dried peas and beans, are not suitable for microwaving as the skins tend to burst during cooking. Split lentils and peas can be microwaved.

Follow these golden rules for successful vegetable cooking:

• Water should be kept to a minimum. A couple of tablespoons sprinkled over is all that is needed. Vegetables are full of liquid. Microwaves make the molecules in this liquid vibrate so the food cooks in its own juice. If you like vegetables on the soft side, add a little more water and extend the cooking time by a few seconds.

• As vegetables are cooked in a minimum amount of water in a microwave, vitamins and minerals are retained and not thrown away when the vegetable is drained.

• Don't use salt before cooking. Microwaved vegetables are packed with flavour so salt isn't always necessary. Sprinkling salt or salted water on to the vegetables before cooking can make the skins tough.

• Vegetables with a high water content, such as mushrooms, courgettes, potatoes, spinach, corn on the cob and cabbage, don't need added water. The water clinging to the vegetables after washing is enough to give good results. At most add 2 tbsp water.

• Always pierce the skin of whole vegetables, such as tomatoes or potatoes, to stop them bursting during cooking.

• Cut vegetables into even-sized pieces. If this is impossible, arrange the vegetables in the dish with the thickest parts towards the outside. If, for instance, you are cooking new potatoes in their skins and some are bigger than others, arrange the larger ones around the outside.

43

- Some potatoes tend to go grey after cooking in the microwave, so for mashed potato it may not be the best cooking method.

- Always cover vegetables with clingfilm or put in a microwave casserole with lid. The exception is baked potatoes, which should be covered with absorbent kitchen paper.

- Stir or shake vegetables at least once during cooking.

- Remember, the fresher and younger the vegetable, the quicker it will cook.

COOKING MORE THAN ONE VEGETABLE

Most meals include more than one vegetable. If you have a divided microwave dish which will hold two or three, start cooking with the vegetable which needs the longest cooking time, then add the others. If, for instance, you were cooking new potatoes, carrots and mange tout you would start with the potatoes, then add the carrots and finish with the mange tout. To compensate for the extra quantity of food (which, of course, affects microwave times), add a minute or so extra at the end of cooking.

DRYING HERBS

If you grow fresh herbs in your garden, it is worth drying some for use in the winter months. Microwave drying is quick and preserves both colour and flavour.

Pick the herbs on a dry day when the dew has evaporated. Remove leaves from stems. Dry about a cupful of herbs at a time. Spread the leaves out on a double thickness of absorbent kitchen paper and cover with two more pieces of paper. Dry the herbs for 4–6 minutes on FULL. The herbs are ready when the leaves are brittle. Leave to cool, then store in an airtight jar. Keep in a dark, cool place.

FRESH VEGETABLES COOKING TIMES

Cooking times are for FULL/HIGH settings unless otherwise stated.
Allow 2–4 minutes standing time after cooking.

ARTICHOKES (GLOBE) MEDIUM

QUANTITY	COOKING TIME IN MINUTES			
	500w	*600/650w*	*700w*	*800/850w*
1	6	5	4½	3½
2	8½	7	6	5
3	13	11	9½	8
4	14½	12	10½	8½

PREPARATION

Remove stalks and trim the tops of the pointed leaves in the usual way.
Put the artichokes in a dish add 5 tbsp water and cover with pierced
clingfilm.

WATCHPOINTS

For even cooking when preparing more than one artichoke, look for
globes of even size. Serve with Hollandaise sauce (page 102) or butter.

ARTICHOKES (JERUSALEM)

QUANTITY	COOKING TIME IN MINUTES			
	500w	*600/650w*	*700w*	*800/850w*
225g (8oz)	5–7	4–6	3½–5	3–4
450g (1lb)	7–9½	6–8	5–7	4–5½

PREPARATION

Peel the artichokes. Slice thickly and sprinkle with lemon juice to
prevent discolouration. Add 2 tbsp water, if liked. Cover with pierced
clingfilm.

WATCHPOINTS

Stir once during cooking. Toss with butter and freshly chopped parsley or purée with cream and a little grated nutmeg.

ASPARAGUS

QUANTITY	COOKING TIME IN MINUTES			
	500w	*600/650w*	*700w*	*800/850w*
225g (8oz)	5	4	3½	3
450g (1lb)	9½	8	7	5½

PREPARATION

Put the asparagus spears in a shallow dish with the thick stalk ends to the outside and the heads to the centre. Add 2–3tbsp water. Cover with pierced clingfilm.

WATCHPOINTS

If some of the spears are much thinner than the others, check shortly before the end of cooking time and remove if cooked. Serve asparagus with melted butter.

AUBERGINES

QUANTITY	COOKING TIME IN MINUTES			
	500w	*600/650w*	*700w*	*800/850w*
225g (8oz) (1 medium)	3½–5	3–4	2½–3½	2–3
450g (1lb)	7–10	6–8	5–7	4–6

PREPARATION

Cut the aubergines into slices about 5mm (¼in) thick. Put the slices in a colander, sprinkle with salt and leave for 30 minutes. Rinse in cold water and pat dry. Arrange in a shallow layer in a dish with the smaller rounds to the centre. Cover with pierced clingfilm.

WATCHPOINTS

Shake halfway through cooking. Use the aubergines to make moussaka, or add canned tomatoes, courgettes, sliced onions, lemon juice and crushed garlic to make ratatouille. For 225g (8oz) aubergines, add three sliced courgettes, one small sliced onion and a small can of tomatoes. Double the quantity for 450g (1lb). Add the extra ingredients 1 minute before the end of cooking time and cook for 2 minutes longer than given for aubergines.

BEANS

BROAD

QUANTITY	COOKING TIME IN MINUTES			
	500w	*600/650w*	*700w*	*800/850w*
225g (8oz)	4	3½	3	2½
450g (1lb)	8½	7	6	5

PREPARATION

Shell. Put in a shallow layer in a dish. Sprinkle with 2–3 tbsp water, depending on amount of beans. Cover with pierced clingfilm.

WATCHPOINTS

Old beans will take longer than young, small ones. Shake or stir at least once during cooking. Served tossed in butter or with 2–3 tbsp double cream and chopped parsley.

FRENCH

QUANTITY	COOKING TIME IN MINUTES			
	500w	*600/650w*	*700w*	*800/850w*
225g (8oz)	8½–9½	7–8	6–7	5–5½
450g (1lb)	17–19	14–16	12–13	10–11

PREPARATION

Trim. Arrange in a shallow layer in a dish with the biggest beans towards the outside. Sprinkle with 2–3 tbsp water, depending on the amount of beans. Cover with pierced clingfilm.

WATCHPOINTS

Serve tossed in butter and freshly chopped parsley.

RUNNER

QUANTITY	COOKING TIME IN MINUTES			
	500w	*600/650w*	*700w*	*800/850w*
225g (8oz)	8½–9½	7–8	6–7	5–5½
450g (1lb)	17–19	14–16	12–13	10–11

PREPARATION

String and cut into even-sized pieces. Arrange in a shallow layer in a dish. Sprinkle with 2–3 tbsp water, depending on amount of beans. Cover with pierced clingfilm.

WATCHPOINTS

Serve as French beans.

BEETROOT

WHOLE BABY

QUANTITY	COOKING TIME IN MINUTES			
	500w	*600/650w*	*700w*	*800/850w*
225g (8oz)	9½–11	8–9	7–8	5½–6½
450g (1lb)	19–21½	16–18	14–15½	12–13½

PREPARATION

Wash well and pierce skins. Arrange in a dish with the biggest beets towards the outside. Note that the biggest suitable beets for cooking whole are about golf ball size. Sprinkle with 2–4 tbsp water, depending on the amount of beetroot. Cover with pierced clingfilm.

WATCHPOINTS

Serve hot, in white sauce or tossed in sour cream and chopped chives. or pickle in vinegar when cold.

SLICED

QUANTITY	COOKING TIME IN MINUTES			
	500w	*600/650w*	*700w*	*800/850w*
225g (8oz)	6–7	5–6	4½–5	3½–4
450g (1lb)	12–14½	10–12	8½–10	7–8½

PREPARATION

Peel and cut into slices. Arrange in a dish so that the biggest slices are towards the outside. Sprinkle with 2–4 tbsp water, depending on the amount of beetroot. Cover with pierced clingfilm.

WATCHPOINTS

Pickle in vinegar when cold. Or serve hot as above. Diced beetroot is good mixed with mayonnaise and chopped onion.

BROCCOLI

QUANTITY	COOKING TIME IN MINUTES			
	500w	*600/650w*	*700w*	*800/850w*
225g (8oz)	5–6	4–5	3½–4	3–3½
450g (1lb)	9½–12	8–10	7–8½	5½–7

PREPARATION

Trim tough stalk ends and outer leaves. Slit stem ends. Arrange in a shallow dish with tough stem ends towards outside and flower heads towards inside. Sprinkle with 2–3 tbsp water. Cover with pierced clingfilm.

WATCHPOINTS

Re-arrange spears during cooking. Serve tossed in butter or with béchamel, mustard, cheese or Hollandaise sauce (page 102).

BRUSSELS SPROUTS

QUANTITY	COOKING TIME IN MINUTES			
	500w	*600/650w*	*700w*	*800/850w*
225g (8oz)	5–6	4–5	3½–4	3–3½
450g (1lb)	9½–12	8–10	7–8½	5½–7

PREPARATION

Discard wilted outer leaves. Trim stalk ends. Cut a cross in stalk ends. Arrange in a shallow layer in a dish with biggest sprouts towards the outside. Sprinkle with 2–4 tbsp water, depending on amount of sprouts. Cover with pierced clingfilm.

WATCHPOINTS

Stir or shake at least once during cooking.

CABBAGE

WHITE AND SAVOY/PRIMO

QUANTITY	COOKING TIME IN MINUTES			
	500w	*600/650w*	*700w*	*800/850w*
225g (8oz)	6–7	5–6	4½–5	3½–4
450g (1lb)	12–14½	10–12	8½–10	7–8½

PREPARATION

Discard yellowed outer leaves. Shred the cabbage, discarding any pieces of tough stalk. Wash the shredded cabbage and shake in a colander; there is no need to use extra water. Place in a shallow layer in a dish and cover with pierced clingfilm.

WATCHPOINTS

Stir the cabbage once or twice during cooking. Toss in butter when cooked and add a little grated nutmeg.

SPRING GREENS

QUANTITY
225g (8oz)
450g (1lb)

COOKING TIME
As for Cabbage

PREPARATION

Discard damaged or wilted outer leaves. Shred the cabbage, making sure you discard tough stalks. Wash the shredded cabbage and shake in a colander; there is no need to use extra water. Place in a shallow layer in a dish and cover with pierced clingfilm.

WATCHPOINTS

Stir once or twice during cooking. Toss in a little butter, or with some chopped crispy bacon.

CARROTS

WHOLE BABY

QUANTITY	**COOKING TIME IN MINUTES**			
	500w	*600/650w*	*700w*	*800/850w*
225g (8oz)	9½–11	8–9	7–8	5½–6½
450g (1lb)	19–21½	16–18	14–15½	11–13

PREPARATION

Only the smallest and most tender baby carrots are suitable for cooking whole. Trim stalk ends. Scrub the carrots. Arrange in a shallow layer in a dish with thickest ends of the carrots towards the outside. Sprinkle with 3–6 tbsp water, depending on the amount of carrots. Cover with pierced clingfilm.

WATCHPOINTS

Toss with freshly chopped parsley or chives and a little butter or double cream. Vinaigrette mixed with chopped fresh herbs is an interesting alternative.

LARGE OR OLD CARROTS

QUANTITY	**COOKING TIME IN MINUTES**			
	500w	*600/650w*	*700w*	*800/850w*
225g (8oz)	8½–9½	7–8	6–7	5–5½
450g (1lb)	17–19	14–16	12–14	10–12

PREPARATION

Scrape or peel and cut into rings. Place in a shallow layer in a dish.

Sprinkle with 2–4 tbsp water, depending on amount of carrots. Cover with pierced clingfilm.

WATCHPOINTS

Toss with a little butter and chopped parsley or chives.

CAULIFLOWER

QUANTITY	COOKING TIME IN MINUTES			
	500w	*600/650w*	*700w*	*800/850w*
225g (8oz)	8½–9½	7–8	6–7	5–5½
450g (1lb)	17–19	14–16	12–14	10–12

PREPARATION

Trim outer green leaves. Divide cauliflower into even-sized florets. Arrange in a shallow layer in a dish, bigger pieces and stalk ends towards the outside. Sprinkle with 2–4 tbsp water, depending on amount of cauliflower. Cover with pierced clingfilm.

WATCHPOINTS

Serve plain, with cheese sauce or polonaise (sprinkled with crisply fried breadcrumbs and sieved hard-boiled egg).

CELERY

HEARTS

QUANTITY	COOKING TIME IN MINUTES			
	500w	*600/650w*	*700w*	*800/850w*
2 medium	12–14½	10–12	8½–10	7–8½

PREPARATION

Cut hearts in half lengthwise. Trim any coarse root. Melt 2 tbsp butter in shallow dish. Toss the hearts in the butter. Sprinkle with 2 tbsp chicken stock per heart. Cover with pierced clingfilm.

WATCHPOINTS

Turn the hearts two or three times during cooking. Boil the stock for 2–3 minutes to reduce it for a sauce.

WHOLE

QUANTITY	COOKING TIME IN MINUTES			
	500w	*600/650w*	*700w*	*800/850w*
medium bunch	9½–12	8–10	7–8½	5½–6

PREPARATION

Divide into sticks. Scrub well. Cut sticks into 5cm (2in) lengths. Toss in a little melted butter, as above. Sprinkle with 4 tbsp chicken stock and cover with pierced clingfilm.

WATCHPOINTS

Stir once or twice during cooking. Reduce stock as above and serve sprinkled with parsley.

CORN ON THE COB

WHOLE COBS

QUANTITY	COOKING TIME IN MINUTES			
	500w	*600/650w*	*700w*	*800/850w*
2	7–9½	6–8	5–7	4–6

PREPARATION

Remove husks. Wash and trim cobs. Wrap the cobs individually in greaseproof paper greased with butter. Arrange around the edge of the turntable or cooking plate. If you want kernels, rather than whole corn, strip from the husk after cooking.

WATCHPOINTS

Serve with plain or flavoured butter. It is best to cook the cobs in twos rather than fours. The first two cobs can be kept warm wrapped tightly in foil while the others cook.

COURGETTES

QUANTITY	COOKING TIME IN MINUTES			
	500w	*600/650w*	*700w*	*800/850w*
225g (8oz)	5½–6½	4½–5½	4–5	3–3½
450g (1lb)	11–13	9–11	8–9½	6½–8

PREPARATION

Wash and slice the courgettes but don't peel them. Arrange in a shallow layer in a dish. Dot with a little butter. There is no need to add water. Cover with pierced clingfilm.

WATCHPOINTS

Stir once or twice during cooking. Serve plain, with chopped herbs or with a garlic-flavoured tomato sauce.

CURLY KALE

QUANTITY	COOKING TIME IN MINUTES			
	500w	*600/650w*	*700w*	*800/850w*
225g (8oz)	5½–6½	4½–5½	4–5	3–3½
450g (1lb)	11–13	9–11	8–9½	6½–8

PREPARATION

Trim thick stalks and chop the leaves roughly as for cabbage or spring greens. Wash and shake well in a colander or dry in a salad spinner. Arrange in a shallow dish. Cover with pierced clingfilm.

WATCHPOINTS

Stir once or twice during cooking. Serve tossed with butter or some crispy bacon pieces.

FENNEL

QUANTITY	COOKING TIME IN MINUTES			
	500w	*600/650w*	*700w*	*800/850w*
1 head	8½–9½	7–8	6–7	5–6
2 heads	12–14	11–13	9½–11	8–9

PREPARATION

Cut each head of fennel into four. Trim any coarse root. Melt 2–4 tbsp butter in a shallow dish. Toss the fennel hearts in the butter. Sprinkle with a little chicken stock. Arrange with the biggest quarters to the outside. Cover with pierced clingfilm.

WATCHPOINTS

Shake the dish once or twice during cooking. If you wish, the fennel can be cooked in slices. To do this, follow the directions for celery hearts on page 51. Serve fennel hearts with cheese sauce.

LEEKS

QUANTITY	COOKING TIME IN MINUTES			
	500w	*600/650w*	*700w*	*800/850w*
225g (8oz)	6–7	5–6	4–5	3½–4
450g (1lb)	9½–12	8–10	7–8½	5½–7

PREPARATION

Trim green tops and roots. Make a cut to about halfway down the white parts of the leeks. Fan leaves under running water to get rid of soil. Either leave the leeks whole if they are small and thin, or cut them into rings. Arrange in a shallow layer in a dish. Sprinkle with a little water. Cover with pierced clingfilm.

WATCHPOINTS

Serve whole leeks plain or with cheese sauce. For a supper dish, wrap each leek in a slice of ham, top with cheese sauce and cook on FULL/HIGH for 2–4 minutes. Turn whole leeks once during cooking. Stir or shake chopped leeks once.

MANGE TOUT

QUANTITY	COOKING TIME IN MINUTES			
	500w	*600/650w*	*700w*	*800/850w*
225g (8oz)	5	4	3½	3
450g (1lb)	9½	8	7	5½

PREPARATION

Pinch the stalk ends off the mange tout. Arrange in a shallow layer in a dish. Cover with pierced clingfilm.

WATCHPOINTS

Shake the dish once or twice during cooking.

MARROW

QUANTITY	COOKING TIME IN MINUTES			
	500w	*600/650w*	*700w*	*800/850w*
225g (8oz)	5½	4½	4	3
450g (1lb)	11	9	8	6½

PREPARATION

Peel and cut into rings 2cm (¾in) thick. Remove the seeds from the centre and cut the rings into quarters. Arrange in a shallow dish and cover with pierced clingfilm.

WATCHPOINTS

Shake once or twice during cooking. Serve with a well flavoured tomato sauce or with cheese sauce.

MUSHROOMS

FLAT, WHOLE

QUANTITY	COOKING TIME IN MINUTES			
	500w	*600/650w*	*700w*	*800/850w*
6	2½–3½	2–3	1½–2½	1½–2

PREPARATION

Trim stalks. Wipe the mushrooms but do not peel them. Arrange, caps down, in a shallow dish. Dot each mushroom with a little butter. Cover with pierced clingfilm.

WATCHPOINTS

Serve mushrooms plain. For a garlic mushroom starter, put ½ tsp garlic butter in each cap before cooking.

BUTTON

QUANTITY	COOKING TIME IN MINUTES			
	500w	*600/650w*	*700w*	*800/850w*
225g (8oz)	2½–3½	2–3	1½–2½	1½–2
450g (1lb)	5–7	4–6	3½–5	3–4

PREPARATION

Leave the mushrooms whole if they are very small. Trim stalks of larger mushrooms and slice in half. Alternatively, slice all mushrooms thinly. Dot with butter and cover with pierced clingfilm. Do not add any water.

WATCHPOINTS

Stir once during cooking. Serve on toast as a savoury or as a light lunch or supper dish.

OKRA

QUANTITY	COOKING TIME IN MINUTES			
	500w	*600/650w*	*700w*	*800/850w*
225g (8oz)	6	5	4	3½
450g (1lb)	12	10	8½	7

PREPARATION

Wash the okra, trim and put in a colander. Sprinkle with salt and leave to drain for 30 minutes. Rinse with cold water and pat dry. Arrange in a shallow dish and cover with pierced clingfilm.

WATCHPOINTS

Shake the dish once or twice during cooking. Turn the okra into an Indian style bhaji by adding a small can of tomatoes to 225g (8oz) and a larger can to 450g (1lb) with some crushed garlic and garam masala powder to taste. Add the tomatoes and juice 1 minute before the end of cooking time.

ONIONS

BABY OR BUTTON

QUANTITY	COOKING TIME IN MINUTES			
	500w	*600/650w*	*700w*	*800/850w*
225g (8oz)	8½–11	7–9	6–8	5–6½
450g (1lb)	17–21½	14–18	12–15½	10–13

PREPARATION

Skin and trim root ends. Arrange in a single layer in a shallow dish, bigger onions towards the outside. Do not add water. Cover with pierced clingfilm.

WATCHPOINTS

Serve baby onions with a white sauce or tossed in butter and freshly chopped parsley. For caramelled baby onions, melt 1 tbsp butter and 1 tbsp brown sugar per 225g (8oz) onions until brown and bubbling. Toss the onions in this mixture.

CHOPPED

QUANTITY	COOKING TIME IN MINUTES			
	500w	*600/650w*	*700w*	*800/850w*
100g (4oz)	4–5½	3½–4½	3–3½	2½–3
225g (8oz)	8½–11	7–9	6–8	5–6½

PREPARATION

Use this method whenever a recipe calls for sautéed onion. Melt 1 tbsp butter per onion in a dish or bowl. Stir in the onions. There is no need to cover.

WATCHPOINTS

Stir the onions once during cooking. Use in casseroles and for other recipes where sautéed onions are needed.

PARSNIPS

QUANTITY	COOKING TIME IN MINUTES			
	500w	*600/650w*	*700w*	*800/850w*
225g (8oz)	3½–4	3–3½	2½–3	2–2½
450g (1lb)	7–8½	6–7	5–6	4–5

PREPARATION

Trim root and stalk ends. Peel. Cut into quarters and remove the hard centre core. Cut remaining pieces into sticks of equal size. Arrange in a shallow layer in a dish. Sprinkle with 2–4 tbsp water, depending on amount of parsnips. Cover with pierced clingfilm.

WATCHPOINTS

Stir or shake parsnips once during cooking. Serve whole or purée with a little butter, cream and grated nutmeg.

PEAS

QUANTITY	COOKING TIME IN MINUTES			
	500w	*600/650w*	*700w*	*800/850w*
225g (8oz)	3½–5	3–4	2½–3½	2–3
450g (1lb)	7–9½	6–8	5–7	4–5½

PREPARATION

Shell. Put in a shallow layer in a dish. Sprinkle with 2–4 tbsp water, depending on amount of peas. Cover with pierced clingfilm.

WATCHPOINTS

Stir or shake once during cooking. Add a sprig of fresh mint and a dot of butter just before the end of cooking.

POTATOES

BAKED

QUANTITY	COOKING
1–4 large	See Watchpoints, over page

PREPARATION

Scrub the potatoes. Prick skins with a fork. Arrange in s circle on a dish or plate and wrap in absorbent kitchen paper.

WATCHPOINTS

Allow 3–4 minutes per potato in an 800/850w oven, 4–5 minutes in 600–700w ovens; 5–6 minutes in 500w oven. Wrap potatoes tightly in foil, with the shiny side inwards, after cooking. Stand for 5 minutes before using.

BOILED, OLD

QUANTITY	COOKING TIME IN MINUTES			
	500w	*600/650w*	*700w*	*800/850w*
225g (8oz)	5–8½	4–7	3½–6	3–5
450g (1lb)	9½–17	8–14	7–12	6–10

PREPARATION

Wash and peel. Cut larger potatoes in half or four so that pieces are even. Put the potatoes in a colander and wash under running water. Put in a dish, arranging larger pieces to the outside. Cover with pierced clingfilm.

WATCHPOINTS

Cooking time will depend on size and type of potato. Toss with butter and chopped parsley. Use cold for potato salad. Use hot for mashed potato. Part cook for roasting.

BOILED, NEW

QUANTITY	COOKING TIME IN MINUTES			
	500w	*600/650w*	*700w*	*800/850w*
225g (8oz)	5–7	4–6	3½–5	3–4
450g (1lb)	9½–14½	8–12	7–10	6–8½

PREPARATION

Wash well but leave potatoes in their skins. Arrange in a dish, bigger potatoes towards the outside. Cover with pierced clingfilm.

WATCHPOINTS

Cooking time will depend on size and type of potato. Toss with butter and chopped parsley. Use cold with vinaigrette and chopped chives.

SORREL

QUANTITY	COOKING TIME IN MINUTES			
	500w	*600/650w*	*700w*	*800/850w*
225g (8oz)	5½–6	3–5	2½–4½	2–3½
450g (1lb)	7–8½	6–7	5–6	4–5

PREPARATION

Remove any wilted leaves or coarse stalks. Wash in several changes of water (as you would for spinach). Put the leaves in a deep dish and cover with pierced clingfilm.

Shake once or twice during cooking. Serve tossed with butter or a little cream.

SPINACH

QUANTITY	COOKING TIME IN MINUTES			
	500w	*600/650w*	*700w*	*800/850w*
225g (8oz)	3½–6	3–5	2½–4½	2–3½
450g (1lb)	7–12	6–10	5–8½	4–7

PREPARATION

Remove any wilted leaves or tough stalks. Wash in several changes of water (this is essential – spinach leaves can be very gritty). Put the leaves into a deep dish. Cover with pierced clingfilm.

WATCHPOINTS

Stir once or twice during cooking. Serve plain, or tossed with butter or a little cream and nutmeg.

SWEDE

QUANTITY	COOKING TIME IN MINUTES			
	500w	*600/650w*	*700w*	*800/850w*
225g (8oz)	5–7	4–6	3½–5	3–4
450g (1lb)	9½–14½	8–12	7–10	6–8½

PREPARATION

Peel. Cut into small even-sized chunks. Wash well. Put in a shallow layer in a dish. Cover with pierced clingfilm.

WATCHPOINTS

Stir once during cooking. Dot with butter just before the end of cooking. Purée or mash to serve.

TOMATOES (LARGE)

QUANTITY	COOKING TIME IN MINUTES			
	500w	*600/650w*	*700w*	*800/850w*
1	2	1½	1	1
2	3½	3	2½	2
3	5½	4½	4	3
4	7	6	5	4

PREPARATION

Cut the tomatoes in half. Melt a little butter in a dish and toss the tomatoes in it. Arrange with cut edges down in a circle around a shallow dish. Or add 2 tbsp water instead of butter. Cover with pierced clingfilm.

WATCHPOINTS

Very ripe tomatoes will cook faster than those which are slightly under-ripe. If you have a glut of tomatoes and want to cook a lot to make purée, skin and seed them first, chop and cook, covered, for 6–8 minutes per 450g (1lb).

TURNIP

NEW, BABY

QUANTITY	COOKING TIME IN MINUTES			
	500w	*600/650w*	*700w*	*800/850w*
225g (8oz)	5–7	4–6	3½–5	3–4
450g (1lb)	9½–14½	8–12	7–10	6–8½

PREPARATION

Trim stalk ends. Peel. Wash well. Cut into quarters if much bigger than golf ball size, otherwise leave whole. Arrange in a shallow dish with biggest turnips to the outside. Cover with pierced clingfilm.

WATCHPOINTS

Stir once during cooking. Dot with butter just before the end of cooking.

OLD, LARGE

QUANTITY	COOKING TIME IN MINUTES			
	500w	*600/650w*	*700w*	*800/850w*
225g (8oz)	8–12	7–10	6–8½	5–7
450g (1lb)	17–24	14–20	12–17	10–14

PREPARATION

Peel and cut into chunks. Wash well. Put in a shallow layer in a dish. Cover with pierced clingfilm.

WATCHPOINTS

Stir once during cooking. Dot with butter just before the end of cooking. Purée or mash to serve. A pinch of grated nutmeg helps to bring out flavour.

FROZEN VEGETABLES COOKING TIMES

Frozen vegetables can be defrosted and cooked on a FULL/HIGH setting in one operation.

● If the vegetables have been frozen in a bag there is no need to use a dish. Simply pierce the bag. Shake or flex the bag during cooking to loosen the contents.

● If the vegetables are in a block, shake or stir once or twice during cooking.

● Home-frozen vegetables take a little longer to defrost/cook than commercially frozen vegetables.

● If you want to cook/defrost more than 225g (8oz) vegetables, do it in two batches. Large amounts do not defrost/cook evenly.

ASPARAGUS

QUANTITY

	COOKING TIME IN MINUTES			
	500w	*600/650w*	*700w*	*800/850w*
one 275g (10oz) pack	9½	8	7	5½

PREPARATION

Put the asparagus in a dish and cover with pierced clingfilm. The stalk ends should be to the outside.

WATCHPOINTS

Separate the asparagus spears after 2–3 minutes.

BEANS

BROAD

QUANTITY

	COOKING TIME IN MINUTES			
	500w	*600/650w*	*700w*	*800/850w*
225g (8oz)	8½–9½	7–8	6–7	5–5½

WATCHPOINTS

Stir or shake during cooking.

FRENCH/RUNNER

QUANTITY
225g (8oz)

COOKING TIME
As for Broad Beans

WATCHPOINTS

Stir or shake during cooking.

BROCCOLI

QUANTITY	**COOKING TIME IN MINUTES**		
	500w	*600/650w*	*700w*	*800/850w*
225g (8oz)	8½–9½	7–8	6–7	5–5½

WATCHPOINTS

Re-arrange spears once halfway through cooking. If in a bag, shake.

BRUSSELS SPROUTS

QUANTITY	**COOKING TIME IN MINUTES**		
	500w	*600/650w*	*700w*	*800/850w*
225g (8oz)	7–9½	6–8	5–7	4–5½

WATCHPOINTS

Stir or shake during cooking.

CARROTS

SLICED

QUANTITY	**COOKING TIME IN MINUTES**		
	500w	*600/650w*	*700w*	*800/850w*
225g (8oz)	7–8½	6–7	5–6	4–5

WATCHPOINTS

Stir or shake during cooking.

CAULIFLOWER

QUANTITY	**COOKING TIME IN MINUTES**		
	500w	*600/650w*	*700w*	*800/850w*
225g (8oz)	8½–11	7–9	6–8	5–6½

WATCHPOINTS

Stir or shake during cooking.

CORN

COB

QUANTITY	COOKING TIME IN MINUTES			
	500w	*600/650w*	*700w*	*800/850w*
1	3½–5	3–4	2½–3½	2–3
2	7–8½	6–7	5–6	4–5

WATCHPOINTS

Wrap in buttered greaseproof paper.

KERNELS

QUANTITY	COOKING TIME IN MINUTES			
	500w	*600/650w*	*700w*	*800/850w*
225g (8oz)	6–7	5–6	4–5	3½–4

WATCHPOINTS

Stir or shake during cooking.

MIXED VEGETABLES

QUANTITY	COOKING TIME IN MINUTES			
	500w	*600/650w*	*700w*	*800/850w*
225g (8oz)	6–7	5–6	4–5	3½–4

WATCHPOINTS

Stir or shake during cooking.

PEAS

QUANTITY	COOKING TIME IN MINUTES			
	500w	*600/650w*	*700w*	*800/850w*
225g (8oz)	6–7	5–6	4–5	3½–4

WATCHPOINTS

Stir or shake during cooking.

SPINACH

CHOPPED

QUANTITY	COOKING TIME IN MINUTES			
	500w	*600/650w*	*700w*	*800/850w*
225g (8oz)	7–9½	6–8	5–7	4–5½

WATCHPOINTS

Do not add water. Stir or shake during cooking.

SWEDE/TURNIP

DICED

QUANTITY	COOKING TIME IN MINUTES			
	500w	*600/650w*	*700w*	*800/850w*
225g (8oz)	7–8½	6–7	5–6	4–5

WATCHPOINTS

Stir or shake during cooking. Stand for 1 minute, then mash with butter, if liked.

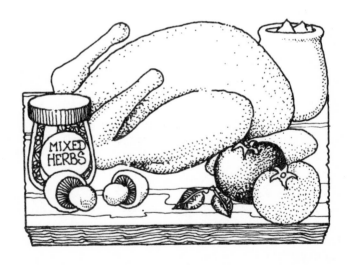

POULTRY AND GAME

Poultry and game cooked by microwave are succulent and full of flavour. The skin does not crisp in the same way as when cooked in a conventional oven, but the quality and flavour of the flesh is better.

● Young, plump chickens and turkeys work best. Older, boiling fowls need to be cooked at a low setting for up to 2 hours, so it isn't really a worthwhile proposition. The only advantage over boiling the bird in a pan is that it can be left unattended – there's no danger of it boiling dry or sticking.

HOW TO ROAST A BIRD

1. Truss the bird well. Wing and leg ends which protrude will char. Protect with small, smooth pieces of foil.

2. Stuff the bird, if liked, put the stuffing in the neck end rather than the cavity. A piece of lemon in the cavity adds flavour.

3. Microwave seasonings can be used to give the skin a brown colour, or paint the bird with 1 tablespoon of warmed honey mixed with 1 teaspoon of Worcestershire sauce. Or any of the suggestions on browning p.11. This gives colour and flavour.
   Using a roasting bag encourages the bird to brown. Roasting bags are available to fit birds up to about 4–5kg (10lb), the biggest which will fit into most microwaves. But for best results, stick to birds 3.5kg (8lb) or less.

4. Put the prepared bird in the roasting bag and secure the bag with a twist tie. The tie must be all plastic, not the type with a flexible metal core. A rubber band will do. Slit the roasting bag to allow juices to drain away (use them for gravy).

5. Put the bag on a rack with a dish beneath (to catch the juices).

6. Cook the bird breast down on FULL/HIGH for the time given in the chart, turning over halfway through cooking.
   When cooking a bird which weighs more than 2.5kg (5lb), allow a standing time of about 20 minutes halfway through cooking.

7. Cover bird with foil shiny side in and leave in the oven.

NOTE: It is very important that poultry be cooked thoroughly. If it isn't, salmonella can multiply in the centre of the bird and cause a nasty attack of food poisoning. As a guide, the centre temperature (through the thickest part between leg and breast) should be 80–85°C (176–185°F) after standing. Test with a meat thermometer.

POULTRY PORTIONS

Poultry portions can be cooked in a roasting bag. Painted with one of the suggested browning agents (see p.11). Frozen portions must be thawed before cooking. Protect bony ends with small, smooth pieces of foil.

CASSEROLING

Poultry is better for long, slow cooking, in the same way as meat casseroles. Remove the skin before casseroling. This encourages flavours to sink into the meat and reduces the fat content.

Rabbit and hare may also be casseroled. For rabbit, adapt any chicken casserole recipe, but hare is best cooked by the long, slow method described in the chart.

GOLDEN RULES FOR COOKING POULTRY AND GAME

• Poultry must be thoroughly thawed before it is microwaved. Poultry with a cold spot at the centre won't cook properly and salmonella may multiply and cause a bad attack of food poisoning.

• When casseroling poultry or game, remove the skin for better flavour and texture.

• Whole birds should be trussed. Protect wing and bone ends with small smooth pieces of foil.

- Stuff the neck rather than the cavity when roasting birds.

- Never salt the skin of poultry before microwaving. Salt draws the moisture away from the flesh.

- Remember the extra standing time half-way through when cooking larger birds.

- When cooking larger birds, the breast and legs may begin to overcook towards the end of cooking time. If this happens, protect with small, smooth pieces of foil.

- Hare should be cooked by the long slow method described on p.72, or it will be tough and unappetising.

If possible, leave a cooked rabbit casserole overnight for the flavours to develop. Re-heat the next day.

DEFROSTING POULTRY

Chicken, turkey and duck must be completely thawed before it is cooked either by microwave or conventional means. Very large birds will start to cook well before thawing is complete, and arriving at an exact thawing time – even with standing – is hit or miss with smaller birds.

Many microwave handbooks will tell you how to defrost poultry completely in a microwave, but it is better for safety's sake to start defrosting in the microwave and to complete the process at room temperature:

Thaw the bird for 2 minutes per 450g (1lb) in the microwave, then complete thawing at room temperature. The bird is properly thawed when the giblets will come away easily from the cavity. This will take from 2–4 hours at room temperature compared to up to 8 hours for thawing without the assistance of a microwave.

If, in an emergency you must defrost a bird totally in the microwave, thaw on WARM/LOW (10 percent power) for 10–20 minutes per 450g (1lb), shielding wing tips and legs with foil. Turn over 2–3 times during thawing and stand for up to 1 hour at end.

- You can thaw poultry portions completely in the microwave. All portions should be thawed on a rack at DEFROST/MED-LOW setting for 6 minutes per 450g (1lb). Wrap portions individually in foil and stand for 15 minutes.

DEFROSTING AND RE-HEATING COOKED POULTRY

Cooked frozen poultry dishes, such as casseroles and Tandoori chicken, can be thawed and re-heated in one operation. Breaded chicken and chicken or turkey pies are not suitable, since the coating or pastry turns soggy. Thawing/re-heating is done on FULL/HIGH.

CASSEROLES

Frozen poultry casseroles can be thawed and re-heated in one operation. Two portions (225g/8oz) meat, plus vegetables: 11 minutes on FULL/HIGH at 500w; 9 minutes at 600/650w; 8 minutes at 700w, 6 ½ minutes at 800/850w. Cover the casserole with clingfilm and break down the edges as it thaws. Move the frozen part at the centre to the edge. Stand, covered in foil, for 5 minutes.

Four portions (450g/1lb) meat, plus vegetables: 20½ minutes at 500w; 17 minutes at 600/650w; 14½ minutes at 700w, 12 minutes at 800/850w. Cover, stir and stand as for the two-portion casserole.

COOKED JOINTS

Frozen cooked chicken joints and Tandoori chicken re-heat well. Put the chicken on a rack and cover with a dome or clingfilm. For two average portions, re-heat on FULL/HIGH for 8½ minutes at 500w; 7 at 600/650w; 6 at 700w, 5 at 800/850w. Wrap tightly in foil and stand for 5 minutes.

For four portions: re-heat on FULL/HIGH for 13 minutes at 500w; 11 at 600/650w; 9½ at 700w 8 at 800/850w. Wrap tightly in foil and stand for 5 minutes.

POULTRY AND GAME COOKING TIME

Times given are for FULL/HIGH setting unless otherwise stated. If your microwave has ROAST/MED-HIGH setting, allow an extra 2 minutes per 450g (1lb).

CHICKEN

WHOLE

QUANTITY	COOKING TIME IN MINUTES PER 450g (1lb)			
	500w	*600/650w*	*700w*	*800/850w*
1–2.5kg (2–5lb)	8½–9½	7–8	6–7	5–5½

PREPARATION

Put half a lemon in the body cavity. Stuff neck end. Truss well. Protect leg and wing tips with small, smooth piece of foil. Paint breast and legs with 1 tbsp warmed honey mixed with 1 tsp Worcestershire sauce or as described on p.11. Put the bird in a roasting bag breast side down on a rack.

STANDING TIME

30 minutes wrapped in foil, shiny side in.

WATCHPOINTS

Turn over half way through cooking. If legs appear to be overcooking towards the end, protect with foil.

PORTIONS

QUANTITY	COOKING TIME IN MINUTES PER 450g (1lb)			
	500w	*600/650w*	*700w*	*800/850w*
450–900g (1–2lb)	8½–9½	7–8	6–7	5–5½

PREPARATION

Paint as for a whole chicken. Protect wing tips and leg ends with small smooth pieces of foil. Put in a single layer in a roasting bag.

STANDING TIME

Wrap individually in foil and stand for 5 minutes.

WHOLE CAPON

QUANTITY	COOKING TIME IN MINUTES PER 450g (1lb)			
	500w	*600/650w*	*700w*	*800/850w*
3–4kg (6–8lb)	8½–9½	7–8	6–7	5–5½

PREPARATION

As for Whole Chicken

STANDING TIME

30 minutes in foil halfway through cooking, then 30 minutes at end.

WATCHPOINTS

As for Whole Chicken. Check centre temperature with a meat thermometer.

WHOLE POUSSIN

QUANTITY	COOKING TIME IN MINUTES PER 450g (1lb)			
	500w	*600/650w*	*700w*	*800/850w*
450–675g (1–1½lb)	8½–9½	7–8	6–7	5–5½

PREPARATION

Protect the bony ends of the legs and wing tips with small, smooth pieces of foil. Put the bird in a roasting bag, breast down on a rack. The breast can be glazed with honey and Worcestershire sauce as described for chicken (page 65) if wished.

STANDING TIME

30 minutes wrapped in foil, shiny side in.

WATCHPOINTS

One poussin can be split down the centre to serve two people. Cook poussins one at a time.

DUCKLING

WHOLE

QUANTITY	COOKING TIME IN MINUTES PER 450g (1lb)			
	500w	*600/650w*	*700w*	*800/850w*
2–2.5kg (4–5lb)	8½–9½	7–8	6–7	5–5½

PREPARATION

Prick flesh all over to allow fat to drain away. Put half an orange in the cavity then continue as for chicken.

STANDING TIME

30 minutes wrapped in foil, shiny side in.

WATCHPOINTS

Drain fat away as duck cooks.

PORTIONS (300g/11oz each)

QUANTITY	COOKING TIME IN MINUTES ON FULL/HIGH THEN SIMMER/MEDIUM			
	500w	*600/650w*	*700w*	*800/850w*
1	4/9½	3½/8	3/7	2½/5½
2	6/15½	5/13	4/11	3½/8
3	9½/31	8/26	7/22½	5½/18½
4	11/37	9/31	8/26½	6½/22

PREPARATION

Prick the skin at intervals to release the fat. Put up to four portions in a roasting bag, skin side down. Protect thin edges or bony parts with small, smooth pieces of foil.

STANDING TIME

10 minutes wrapped in foil, shiny side in.

WATCHPOINTS

Microwaved duck does not have crispy skin like the oven roasted variety. To crisp the skin after cooking, sear it under a hot grill.

GUINEA FOWL

Cook exactly as described for Chicken.

HARE

JOINTED

QUANTITY	COOKING TIME IN MINUTES ON FULL/HIGH			
	500w	*600/650w*	*700w*	*800/850w*
1 average-sized hare	7	6	5	4

PREPARATION

Cut the joints into small pieces, taking as much meat away from the
bone as possible. Marinate for 24 hours in a mixture of 3 tbsp olive oil,
4 tbsp port, a chopped onion and some black pepper.

Remove the hare from the marinade and dab dry with absorbent
kitchen paper. Brush with melted butter. Put in a microwave-safe
casserole dish and cover with pierced clingfilm. Cook on FULL/HIGH
for the times given above.

THE NEXT STAGE

Lift the hare pieces out of the dish. Stir 1 tbsp plain flour into the
juices and half a bottle of red wine or port. Bring to the boil on FULL/
HIGH, stir well, then return the hare pieces to the dish. Cook on
DEFROST/MED-LOW as follows:

COOKING TIME IN MINUTES ON MED/LOW			
500w	*600/650w*	*700w*	*800/850w*
82	68	58	48

THE NEXT STAGE

Add a few button onions and a peeled and crushed garlic clove and
continue to cook on WARM/LOW for another 30 minutes on all
microwaves. Add a few mushrooms 5 minutes before the end of cooking.

WATCHPOINTS

This long, slow cooking method is the only way to cook hare in a
microwave. Faster cooking results in tough, unappetising meat.

PARTRIDGE

QUANTITY	COOKING TIME IN MINUTES PER 450g (1lb)			
	500w	*600/650w*	*700w*	*800/850w*
2 average-sized ovenready birds	14½	12	10½	8½

PREPARATION

Stuff the partridges with the stuffing of your choice. Truss well. Weigh. Protect bony leg ends and wing tips with small smooth pieces of foil. Put the birds in a large roasting bag, breast down on a rack. Slit the bag to allow juices to drain away.

STANDING TIME

15 minutes wrapped in foil, shiny side in.

WATHCPOINTS

To cook just one bird, halve the cooking times given here. Use the juices to make gravy.

PHEASANT

QUANTITY	COOKING TIME IN MINUTES PER 450g (1lb)			
	500w	*600/650w*	*700w*	*800/850w*
1 average-sized bird (750g–1.5kg/1¾–3lb)	14½	12	10½	8½

PREPARATION

Put an onion and bayleaf in cavity for flavour. Protect bony wing tips and leg ends with small, smooth pieces of foil. Put the bird in a roasting bag and cook breast down on a rack. Slit the bag to allow juices to drain away.

STANDING TIME

15 minutes wrapped in foil, shiny side in.

WATCHPOINTS

Use the juices to make gravy. Add a little port, if liked. If cooking a brace of pheasants, cook one at a time.

RABBIT

JOINTED

QUANTITY	COOKING TIME ON SIMMER/MEDIUM
675g (1½lb)	(same for all ovens) 50–60 minutes until the meat is tender. Stir once or twice during cooking. Stand for 5 minutes.

PREPARATION

Cut the rabbit into serving pieces and sauté in melted butter for

6 minutes on FULL/HIGH. Add the vegetables of your choice cut in even-sized pieces, plus stock but if using mushrooms, leave these to 5 minutes before the end of cooking time.

TURKEY

WHOLE

QUANTITY	COOKING TIME IN MINUTES PER 450g (1lb)			
	500w	*600/650w*	*700w*	*800/850w*
3–5kg (6–10lb)	7–9½	6–8	5–7	4–5½

PREPARATION

As for Chicken

STANDING TIME

30 minutes halfway through, then 30 minutes at end.

WATCHPOINTS

As for Chicken. If breast starts to overcook, protect.

PORTIONS

QUANTITY	COOKING TIME IN MINUTES PER 450g (1lb)			
	500w	*600/650w*	*700w*	*800/850w*
1–25kg (2–2½lb)	8½–9½	7–8	6–7	5–5½

PREPARATION

As for Chicken portions

STANDING TIME

Wrap individually in foil and stand for 5 minutes.

ROLL

QUANTITY	COOKING TIME IN MINUTES PER 450g (1lb)			
	500w	*600/650w*	*700w*	*800/850w*
1–2kg (2–4lb)	11–12	9–10	8–8½	6½–7

PREPARATION

Put in a roasting bag on a rack as for whole birds but do not paint with a browning agent.

STANDING TIME

Turn over halfway through cooking, then stand wrapped in foil for 5 minutes. Stand for 20 minutes at end.

BREAST JOINT

QUANTITY	COOKING TIME IN MINUTES PER 450g (1lb)			
	500w	*600/650w*	*700w*	*800/850w*
1–2kg (2–4lb)	9½	8	7	5½

PREPARATION

Paint skin with browning agent as for whole chicken. Put in a roasting bag as for whole chicken.

STANDING TIME

Turn over halfway through cooking, then stand wrapped in foil for 5 minutes. Stand for 20 minutes at end.

WATCHPOINTS

Turn over twice during cooking.

WOOD PIGEON

QUANTITY	COOKING TIME IN HOURS ON DEFROST/MED-LOW			
	500w	*600/650w*	*700w*	*800/850w*
225g (8oz) maximum, two birds at a time	2	1¾	1½	1–1¼

PREPARATION

Brush the pigeons with melted butter, cover and cook for 5 minutes, on FULL/HIGH, turning once. If cooking one bird, cook for 2 minutes. Sauté a little onion and some chopped bacon in the juices. Stir 1 tbsp plain flour and half a bottle of red wine into the juices. Cook on FULL/HIGH for 3–4 minutes until thickened, stirring every minute. Return the pigeons to the dish, making sure they are covered by the sauce (if not, add more stock or wine). Cover with pierced clingfilm. Cook on DEFROST/MED-LOW for the times given above.

WATCHPOINTS

Baste with sauce from time to time. Add mushrooms 5 minutes before the end of cooking time. For one pigeon, halve the times given here.

FISH AND SHELLFISH

Good, fresh fish is subtly flavoured and deliciously tender – qualities
which can be destroyed when cooked by some conventional methods.
Microwaving cooks fish without over-softening the delicate flesh, or
ruining the flavour.

● Any fish which would normally be steamed, baked or boiled is very
good microwaved, as the fish can be cooked without the addition of
liquid. All that's needed is a dash of lemon juice, a little butter and a
grinding of black pepper.

● If you are making a fish dish which would normally have a sauce, the
fish can be microwaved poached in milk, wine or stock and the resulting
flavour-packed liquid used to make a sauce.

● Most shellfish is sold ready cooked. Do not try to cook a live lobster
or crab by microwave – use the traditional plunge into boiling water
instead. Fresh prawns etc. can be cooked in their shells.

● Mussels can be microwaved, but check them carefully first. Discard
any which seem either very heavy or very light for their size as the
shell may be full of either water or sand.

● All types of smoked fish can be cooked in the microwave. Frozen
pre-packed boil-in-the-bag fish is especially good.

● Don't microwave breadcrumbed fish, since the coating turns soggy
(unless you use a browning dish). Likewise, frying should not be
attempted in a microwave.

GOLDEN RULES FOR COOKING FISH

● Fish should always be covered during cooking to keep it moist and
reduce cooking smells!

● Brush around the hollow centre bones of fish cutlets with a little
lemon juice. This will prevent spattering.

- Arrange fillets with tails overlapping or turn the tails underneath the fish so that thickness is even.

- If cooking a whole fish, protect the tail end with a small piece of smooth foil.

- Slit the skin of large pieces of fish or whole fish to prevent bursting.

- Test the fish before the end of cooking time; it can easily overcook.

- Don't microwave crumbed or battered fish. The coating turns soggy.

- Don't try to cook a whole live crab or lobster in the microwave.

- Cook large fish in a roasting bag. Be sure it is long enough to allow space at each end of the fish. Pierce the bag before cooking.

- Always brush delicate white fish with melted butter or olive oil and a little lemon juice.

- If preparing a fish dish with a sauce, cook the fish in the liquid needed for the sauce, then use this as stock.

- Fish should be turning opaque at end of microwaving. It will complete cooking during standing time. If patches still look translucent after standing, cook a few seconds longer.

FROZEN FISH

- For best results fish and shellfish should be completely thawed before cooking. If still frozen at the centre, it won't cook evenly.

- Fish is always defrosted on DEFROST/MEDIUM-LOW in short bursts with standing time to ensure that the flesh thaws rather than cooks.

- Like meat, fish should be put on a rack for defrosting, so that the liquid given out drips away from the flesh.

- The fish should always be covered, either with clingfilm or with a plastic dome. A dome is more convenient as it is quick to remove when frozen fillets have to be separated or pieces of fish moved around.

- Fish fillets should be separated as soon as possible. The tail ends must then be protected with small, smooth pieces of foil.

- Whole fish can be thawed in their wrapping, but protect the head and tail with foil halfway through thawing.

- Shellfish, such as prawns and scampi, can be thawed on or off the shell in the freezer wrapping. It is not advisable to thaw lobster or crab in the microwave.

• Keep a close eye on the fish during thawing. It should stay cold. If the fish starts to warm up, remove it from the microwave and complete thawing naturally.

• Cooked fish dishes in sauce can be re-heated from frozen. Use a ROAST/MED-HIGH setting so that the fish and sauce heat up at the same rate.

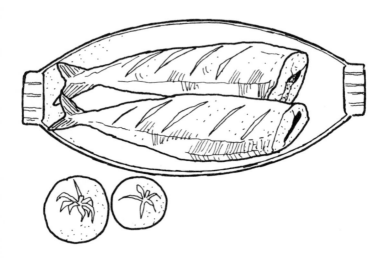

FISH THAWING TIMES

Fish is thawed on DEFROST/MED-LOW/30 percent. The time is the same for all microwaves as power levels differ very little at this low setting. Stand wrapped in foil.

COD

FILLETS

QUANTITY	DEFROST TIME	STANDING TIME
225g (8oz)	3 minutes	5 minutes
450g (lb)	5–6 minutes	5 minutes

WATCHPOINTS

Check that tail ends stay cool. Separate fillets as soon as possible.

STEAKS/CUTLETS

QUANTITY	DEFROST TIME	STANDING TIME
225g (8oz)	3 minutes	5 minutes
450g (lb)	5–6 minutes	5 minutes

SMOKED FILLETS

QUANTITY	DEFROST TIME	STANDING TIME
225g (8oz)	3 minutes	5 minutes
450g (lb)	5–6 minutes	5 minutes

WATCHPOINTS

Check that tail ends stay cool. Separate fillets as soon as possible.

HADDOCK

FILLETS

QUANTITY	DEFROST TIME	STANDING TIME
225g (8oz)	3 minutes	5 minutes
450g (lb)	5–6 minutes	5 minutes

WATCHPOINTS

Check that tail ends stay cool. Separate fillets as soon as possible.

STEAKS/CUTLETS

QUANTITY	DEFROST TIME	STANDING TIME
225g (8oz)	3 minutes	5 minutes
450g (lb)	5–6 minutes	5 minutes

HAKE CUTLETS

QUANTITY	DEFROST TIME	STANDING TIME
225g (8oz)	3 minutes	5 minutes
450g (lb)	5–6 minutes	5 minutes

HERRING

KIPPER

QUANTITY	COOKING TIME ON FULL
1	4–5 minutes

STANDING TIME

1 minute

WATCHPOINTS

Don't thaw first. Cook in a bag when frozen.

WHOLE

QUANTITY	DEFROST TIME	STANDING TIME
2	6–8 minutes	5 minutes

WATCHPOINTS

Protect head and tail with foil halfway through thawing.

MACKEREL

WHOLE

As for Herring

PLAICE

FILLET

QUANTITY	DEFROST TIME	STANDING TIME
225g (8oz)	2–3 minutes	5 minutes
450g (lb)	4–5 minutes	5 minutes

WATCHPOINTS

Check that tail ends stay cool.

SALMON

STEAKS

DEFROST TIME
2 minutes per steak

STANDING TIME
5 minutes per steak

SALMON TROUT

WHOLE

QUANTITY
one 900g (2lb) fish

**DEFROST/
STANDING
TIME**
Thaw for 10 minutes
then stand for 20
minutes. Thaw for
another 5 minutes and
stand for 30 minutes.

WATCHPOINTS

Protect head and tail with foil for second part of thawing.

SOLE

WHOLE

QUANTITY
one 225g (8oz) fish

DEFROST TIME
4 minutes

STANDING TIME
5 minutes

WATCHPOINTS

Thaw for 4 minutes per fish. Protect head and tail with foil halfway
through thawing.

TROUT

WHOLE

QUANTITY
one 225g (8oz) fish

DEFROST TIME
4 minutes

STANDING TIME
5 minutes

WATCHPOINTS

Thaw for 4 minutes per average fish. Protect head and tail with foil halfway through thawing.

FISH AND SHELLFISH COOKING TIMES

Cooking times are for FULL/HIGH settings unless otherwise stated.

COD

FILLETS

QUANTITY	COOKING TIME IN MINUTES			
	500w	*600/650w*	*700w*	*800/850w*
225g (8oz)	2½–3	2–2½	1½–2	1½
450g (1lb)	4–5	3½–4	3–3½	2½–3

PREPARATION

Arrange in a single layer in a dish, thick edges to outside, tails overlapping. Brush the fish with melted butter and sprinkle with lemon juice. For extra flavour, use melted garlic, maître d'hôtel, lemon, orange or mustard butter. Cover with pierced clingfilm.

STANDING TIME

5 minutes

WATCHPOINTS

Check fish before end of cooking time. If tail ends start to dry out, cover with foil. Clingfilm is fine for standing time.

STEAKS/CUTLETS

QUANTITY	COOKING TIME IN MINUTES			
	500w	*600/650w*	*700w*	*800/850w*
225g (8oz)	2½–3	2–2½	1½–2	1½
450g (1lb)	4–5	3½–4	3–3½	2½–3

PREPARATION

Arrange in a dish. Brush around centre bone with lemon juice. Alternatively, remove the centre bone and stuff the cavity with chopped mushrooms tossed in melted butter, or with skinned, chopped tomatoes flavoured with basil. Cover with pierced clingfilm.

STANDING TIME

5 minutes

WATCHPOINTS

Check fish before end of cooking time.

SMOKED FILLETS

QUANTITY	COOKING TIME IN MINUTES			
	500w	*600/650w*	*700w*	*800/850w*
225g (8oz)	2½–3	2–2½	1½–2	1½
450g (1lb)	4–5	3½–4	3–3½	2½–3

PREPARATION

Lay fillets in a dish. Overlap tails. If there is only one fillet, turn the tail under with fish skin side down. Pour enough milk over the fish almost to cover it. Add a knob of butter.

STANDING TIME

5 minutes

WATCHPOINTS

Check fish before end of cooking time. Serve fish alone or with poached eggs. Retain liquid, strain, cool and freeze for future use as fish stock. For a delicious fish pie, flake fish and use liquid to make cheese sauce. Mix fish and sauce. Put in a dish. Top with sliced hard-boiled eggs and puff pastry. Finish off in a conventional oven.

PRE-PACKED BOIL-IN-THE-BAG

QUANTITY	COOKING TIME IN MINUTES			
	500w	*600/650w*	*700w*	*800/850w*
one 225g (8oz) bag	6	5	4	3½

PREPARATION

These packs come in various sizes. Follow maker's microwave instructions if the pack has them. Otherwise, pierce the frozen bag and place on a plate.

STANDING TIME

5 minutes

WATCHPOINTS

Shake bag gently once or twice as fish thaws and cooks.

HADDOCK

FILLETS

QUANTITY	COOKING TIME IN MINUTES			
	500w	*600/650w*	*700w*	*800/850w*
225g (8oz)	2½–3	2–2½	1½–2	1½
450g (1lb)	4–5	3½–4	3–3½	2½–3

PREPARATION

Arrange in a single layer, thick edges to outside, tails overlapping.
Brush the fish with melted butter and sprinkle with lemon juice.

STANDING TIME

5 minutes

WATCHPOINTS

Check tail ends before end of cooking time. Cover with a small piece of
foil if needed.

STEAKS/CUTLETS

QUANTITY	COOKING TIME IN MINUTES			
	500w	*600/650w*	*700w*	*800/850w*
225g (8oz)	2½–3	2–2½	1½–2	1½
450g (1lb)	4–5	3½–4	3–3½	2½–3

PREPARATION

Brush around the centre bone with lemon juice. Alternatively, remove
centre bone and stuff cavity, as for cod steaks. Brush the fish with
melted butter. Cover with pierced clingfilm.

STANDING TIME

5 minutes

WATCHPOINTS

Check fish before end of cooking time.

SMOKED FILLETS

As for Smoked Cod

PRE-PACKED BOIL-IN-THE-BAG

As for Cod

HAKE

STEAKS/CUTLETS

QUANTITY	COOKING TIME IN MINUTES			
	500w	*600/650w*	*700w*	*800/850w*
225g (8oz)	2½–3	2–2½	1½–2	1½
450g (1lb)	4–5	3½–4	3–3½	2½–3

PREPARATION

Place in a single layer in a dish. Brush with melted butter and a little lemon juice. Cover with pierced clingfilm.

STANDING TIME

5 minutes

WATCHPOINTS

Check fish before end of cooking time. Serve hot with parsley sauce.

HERRING

KIPPERS

QUANTITY	COOKING TIME IN MINUTES PER 225g (8oz)			
	500w	*600/650w*	*700w*	*800/850w*
1	3½	3	2½	2

PREPARATION

Cook one kipper at a time. Put on a rack, skin side down. Brush with melted butter. Cover with greaseproof paper.

STANDING TIME

5 minutes

WATCHPOINTS

Turn the kipper over when it begins to curl.

WHOLE

QUANTITY	COOKING TIME IN MINUTES PER 450g (1lb)			
	500w	*600/650w*	*700w*	*800/850w*
1–2	6	5	4	3½

PREPARATION

Gut and scale fish. Trim fins. Wash cavity and season with black pepper and lemon juice. For extra flavour, stuff each fish with mixture of 2 tbsp brown breadcrumbs, 1 tbsp chopped apple and the zest of half a lemon, or with any stuffing recommended for oily fish. Weigh. Cook fish individually in bags, or wrapped in greaseproof paper.

STANDING TIME

8 minutes

WATCHPOINTS

Keep the fish wrapped in greaseproof paper for standing. Check tail, and cover with foil if it is drying out.

BOIL-IN-THE-BAG KIPPER FILLETS

QUANTITY	COOKING TIME IN MINUTES			
	500w	*600/650w*	*700w*	*800/850w*
225g (8oz)	2½–3	2–2½	1½–2	1½
450g (1lb)	4–5	3½–4	3–3½	2½–3

PREPARATION

Pierce the bag. Stand on a rack or follow manufacturer's instructions.

STANDING TIME

5 minutes

WATCHPOINTS

Shake bag gently as food thaws/cooks.

MACKEREL

WHOLE

QUANTITY	COOKING TIME IN MINUTES PER 450g (1lb)			
	500w	*600/650w*	*700w*	*800/850w*
1–2	6	5	4	3½

PREPARATION AND STANDING

As for Whole herring

WATCHPOINTS

As for Whole herring.

MUSSELS

QUANTITY	COOKING TIME IN MINUTES			
	500w	*600/650w*	*700w*	*800/850w*
1 litre (2pt)	5–7	4–6	3½–5	3–4
2 litres (4pt)	9½–14½	8–12	7–10	5½–8½

PREPARATION

Look for good-sized mussels. The best are available from September until March–April. Soak them in a bucket of water for at least four hours. Change the water two or three times. Scrape away 'beards' and any barnacles. Discard any with broken shells or which do not close when tapped.

Melt 1–2 tbsp butter in a large, shallow bowl on FULL/HIGH. Add a finely chopped onion, 1 crushed garlic clove, ½–1 bottle dry white wine and the mussels. Cover with pierced clingfilm.

WATCHPOINTS

Toss well halfway through cooking. The mussels are cooked when they are open. Discard any which do not open. Stir some double cream if liked, into the cooking juices sprinkle with chopped parsley and serve with the mussels. Serve French bread to mop up the delicious sauce.

PLAICE

FILLETS

QUANTITY	COOKING TIME IN MINUTES PER 450g (1lb)			
	500w	*600/650w*	*700w*	*800/850w*
225g (8oz)	2½–3	2–2½	1½–2	1½
450g (1lb)	4–5	3½–4	3–3½	2½–3

PREPARATION

Lay in a single layer in a dish, tails overlapping, skin side down. Brush fish with melted butter and lemon juice. Cover with clingfilm.

STANDING TIME

5 minutes

WATCHPOINTS

Check tails before end of cooking. Cover with foil if needed. Serve fish plain or with a sauce.

WHOLE – See sole p.90.

SALMON

STEAKS (100g/4oz each)

QUANTITY	COOKING TIME IN MINUTES			
	500w	*600/650w*	*700w*	*800/850w*
2	5	4	3½	3
4	9½	8	7	5½

PREPARATION

Brush around the centre bone of the fish with lemon juice. Brush flesh
with butter. Pour half a glass of dry white wine over two steaks, a
whole glass over four. Cover with pierced clingfilm.

STANDING TIME

6 minutes

WATCHPOINTS

Serve steaks hot with maître d'hôtel butter or Hollandaise sauce, or
cold with mayonnaise.

SALMON TROUT

WHOLE SMALL

QUANTITY	COOKING TIME IN MINUTES			
	500w	*600/650w*	*700w*	*800/850w*
900g (2lb)	12	10	8½	7

PREPARATION

Slash the skin of the fish at intervals. Brush the fish with butter and
lemon juice. Place the fish in a cooking bag with a quarter of a lemon.
Pierce bag. Put the bag on a rack.

STANDING TIME

8 minutes

WATCHPOINTS

Check tail before end of cooking and cover with foil if needed. Serve
fish hot with Hollandaise sauce or leave until cold, skin and decorate
with aspic or very thin cucumber slices and serve with mayonnaise.

SCAMPI

NATURAL

QUANTITY	COOKING TIME IN MINUTES			
	500w	*600/650w*	*700w*	*800/850w*
225g (8oz)	2	1½	1–1½	1
450g (1lb)	3½	3	2½	2

PREPARATION

Use this method for scampi off the shell to be served with a sauce. Place the fish in a shallow dish. Pour a small glass of dry white wine over 225g (8oz), a larger glass over 450g (1lb). Season with black pepper, add a knob of butter and cover with pierced clingfilm.

STANDING TIME

4 minutes

WATCHPOINTS

Shake once or twice during cooking. Use liquid as a base for sauce.

SOLE

WHOLE

QUANTITY	COOKING TIME IN MINUTES			
	500w	*600/650w*	*700w*	*800/850w*
one 225g (8oz) fish	2½	2	1½–2	1½
450g (1lb) fish	5	4	3½	3

PREPARATION

Skin the fish. Brush with melted butter and lemon juice. Protect tail with a small piece of smooth foil. Cook one fish at a time in a shallow dish. Cover with pierced clingfilm.

STANDING TIME

5 minutes

WATCHPOINTS

Check tail, and cover with foil if it starts to overcook.

TROUT

WHOLE

QUANTITY	COOKING TIME IN MINUTES			
	500w	*600/650w*	*700w*	*800/850w*
one 225g (8oz) fish	8½	7	6	5

PREPARATION

Brush the fish with melted butter and lemon juice. Protect tail with a small piece of smooth foil. Place the fish in a roasting bag. Pierce the bag and put it on a rack. Cook up to two fish at a time.

STANDING TIME

5 minutes

WATCHPOINTS

Turn the bag over halfway through cooking time. Serve sprinkled with toasted flaked almonds.

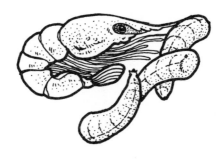

FRUIT

With so many stone and berry fruits available all the year round, it is quick and simple to prepare a delicious dessert with the help of your microwave.

Both fresh and dried fruits microwave well and can be used as a base for steamed puddings and crumbles, ice creams, sauces and purées. As with vegetables, fruits retain a high percentage of their flavour and colour when cooked in a microwave oven.

PREPARING FRUITS FOR MICROWAVING

● Hard fruits, such as apples and pears, should be peeled and cored in the usual way.

● Cut the fruit into even-sized pieces and sprinkle with sugar to taste. There is no need to add liquid – the fruit will cook in its own juice.

● Plums, cherries, greengages and damsons should be halved and stoned (or cherries can be left whole if you have a cherry stoner).

● Peaches and apricots don't need skinning before you microwave, the skins will peel away afterwards.

● Cut the fruit in half, remove the stones and sprinkle with sugar to taste.

● Vanilla sugar (sugar flavoured by being stored in a jar with a vanilla pod) adds delicious flavour.

● Berry fruits, such as red and black currants and gooseberries, cook particularly well in the microwave. Top, tail and wash the fruit in the usual way, then add sugar to taste.

FROZEN FRUIT

Frozen fruits can be partly defrosted in the microwave, then left to defrost naturally. Long microwaving means that the outside of the fruits will begin to cook, so natural thawing is essential.

- Free flow frozen fruit (usually commercially frozen): best thawed naturally.

- Fruit home-frozen in dry sugar: allow 2 minutes per 225g (8oz)/4 minutes per 450g (1lb) at FULL/HIGH on all wattages, then leave to thaw naturally.

- Fruit home-frozen in syrup: allow 4 minutes per 225g (8oz)/8 minutes per 450g (1lb) at FULL/HIGH on all wattages, then leave to thaw naturally.

- Frozen fruit purée: allow 2 minutes per 225g (8oz)/4 minutes per 450g (1lb) at FULL/HIGH on all wattages, then leave to thaw naturally.

DRIED FRUITS

Dried fruit can be plumped/cooked in one operation using the microwave. There is no need for overnight soaking. The maximum amount of fruit which can be cooked at one time is 225g (8oz).

- Put the fruit in a bowl, add enough water, wine, fruit juice or cold strained tea to cover.

- Microwave on FULL/HIGH for 7 minutes at *500w*; 6 minutes at *600/650w*; 5 minutes at *700w*; 4 minutes at *800/850w*. Stand, covered with foil, for 5 minutes, then use hot or cold as needed.

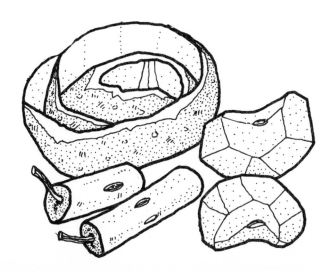

FRUIT COOKING TIMES

Times given are for FULL/HIGH setting unless otherwise stated.
Leave to stand for 2 minutes after cooking.

APPLES, COOKING

SLICES OR PURÉE

QUANTITY	COOKING TIME IN MINUTES			
	500w	*600/650w*	*700w*	*800/850w*
225g (8oz)	3½–5	3–4	2½–3½	2–3
450g (1lb)	7–9½	6–8	5–7	4–5½

PREPARATION

For cooked apple slices, peel and core apple and slice thinly. Lay in a
shallow layer in a dish. Sprinkle with sugar to taste and add a little
cinnamon if wished. Add a few flakes of butter for extra rich slices, or
for purée. Cover with pierced clingfilm.

WATCHPOINTS

Gently stir once or twice during cooking. Use as the base for a
crumble, or purée the fruit. Lemon or orange zest adds extra flavour.

BAKED

QUANTITY	COOKING TIME IN MINUTES			
	500w	*600/650w*	*700w*	*800/850w*
2	6	5	4	3½
4	12	10	8½–9	7

PREPARATION

For baked apples, core the apples. Stuff each core with 1 tbsp brown
sugar mixed with ½ tbsp dried fruit and a pinch of cinnamon, or fill
with mincemeat. Mark around the diameter of each apple with a sharp
knife. This will prevent the skin from bursting. Put the apples in a
dish. If there are four, arrange the fruit in a circle. Do not cover.

94

WATCHPOINTS

Watch apples as they cook. When the band of green around the centre has reduced to about 6mm (¼in) remove the apples from the microwave. Cover with clingfilm and wait for 5 minutes. The band of green will disappear.

BANANAS

QUANTITY	COOKING TIME IN MINUTES			
	500w	*600/650w*	*700w*	*800/850w*
2	7	6	5	4

PREPARATION

Peel. Cut into slices lengthwise and arrange in a shallow layer in a dish. Sprinkle with 1 tsp brown sugar per banana. Add the zest and juice of an orange for delicious flavour. Cover the dish with pierced clingfilm.

WATCHPOINTS

Remove clingfilm towards the end of cooking. Add 25g (1oz) dried fruit and a knob of butter for a rich dessert. Serve with cream.

BLACKBERRIES

QUANTITY	COOKING TIME IN MINUTES			
	500w	*600/650w*	*700w*	*800/850w*
225g (8oz)	2–3	1½–2½	1–2	1–1½
450g (1lb)	3½–6	3–5	2½–4	2–3½

PREPARATION

Wash fruit. Place in a shallow layer in a dish. Sprinkle with sugar to taste. Cover with pierced clingfilm.

WATCHPOINTS

Stir the berries gently once or twice during cooking. Use as a base for a crumble or sponge pudding, or serve with cream or custard.

BLACKCURRANTS

QUANTITY	COOKING TIME IN MINUTES			
	500w	*600/650w*	*700w*	*800/850w*
225g (8oz)	2–3	1½–2½	1–2	1–1½
450g (1lb)	3½–6	3–5	2½–4	2–3½

PREPARATION

String fruit. Wash. Shake in a colander. Place in a shallow layer in a dish. Sprinkle with sugar to taste. Cover with pierced clingfilm.

WATCHPOINTS

Stir or shake gently once or twice during cooking. Use as a base for a crumble or sponge pudding, or serve cold with cream or ice cream.

CHERRIES

QUANTITY	COOKING TIME IN MINUTES			
	500w	*600/650w*	*700w*	*800/850w*
225g (8oz)	2½–3½	2–3	2–2½	1½–2
450g (1lb)	5–6	4–5	3½–4	3–3½

PREPARATION

Stone the fruit, using a cherry stoner. Lay in a shallow layer in a dish. Sprinkle with sugar to taste if needed. Cover with pierced clingfilm.

WATCHPOINTS

Stir or shake gently once or twice during cooking. Serve cold with ice cream or whipped fresh cream.

DAMSONS

QUANTITY	COOKING TIME IN MINUTES			
	500w	*600/650w*	*700w*	*800/850w*
225g (8oz)	2½–3½	2–3	2–2½	1½–2
450g (1lb)	5–6	4–5	3½–4	3–3½

PREPARATION

Wash the fruit. Split and remove stones. Lay cut side up in a shallow dish. Sprinkle with sugar to taste. Cover with pierced clingfilm.

WATCHPOINTS

Stir once during cooking to coat the fruit with juice. Use as the base for a crumble or sponge pudding, or serve hot or cold with cream or custard.

GOOSEBERRIES

QUANTITY

	COOKING TIME IN MINUTES			
	500w	*600/650w*	*700w*	*800/850w*
225g (8oz)	5	4	3½	3
450g (1lb)	9½	8	7	5½

PREPARATION

Top and tail. Place in dish. Sprinkle with sugar to taste. Cover with pierced clingfilm.

WATCHPOINTS

Stir or shake gently once or twice during cooking.

GREENGAGES

QUANTITY

	COOKING TIME			
	500w	*600/650w*	*700w*	*800/850w*
225g (8oz)	2½–3½	2–3	2–2½	1½–2
450g (1lb)	5–6	4–5	3½–4	3–3½

PREPARATION

As for Damsons

WATCHPOINTS

As for Damsons

LEMONS

QUANTITY

	COOKING TIME			
	500w	*600/650w*	*700w*	*800/850w*
1	1 min	50 secs	40 secs	30 secs

PREPARATION

To extract the juice from a lemon, cut the fruit in half. Position, cut side down, on a dish. Cover with pierced clingfilm.

WATCHPOINTS

As the lemon heats up, the juice will flow from the flesh, leaving the pith and pips behind. Cool juice before use.

ORANGES

QUANTITY

	COOKING TIME			
	500w	*600/650w*	*700w*	*800/850w*
1	1 min	50 secs	40 secs	30 secs

PREPARATION

To extract the juice from an orange, treat as for Lemons.

WATCHPOINTS

As for Lemons

PEACHES

QUANTITY

	COOKING TIME IN MINUTES			
	500w	*600/650w*	*700w*	*800/850w*
2	2½	2	1½–2	1½
4	5	4	3½	3

PREPARATION

Wash. Halve and stone. Place, cut sides up, in a shallow dish. Sprinkle with sugar if needed. Cover with pierced clingfilm.

WATCHPOINTS

Slip skins from fruit after cooking. Peaches can also be cooked in slices. Cooking time is the same. Use hot, cold or puréed.

PEARS

QUANTITY

	COOKING TIME IN MINUTES			
	500w	*600/650w*	*700w*	*800/850w*
225g (8oz)	5½–7	4½–6	4–5	3–4
450g (1lb)	11–14½	9–12	8–10	6½–8½

PREPARATION

Wash. Peel, halve and core. Cut into quarters or slices. Sprinkle with sugar to taste and a little cinnamon. Cover with pierced clingfilm.

WATCHPOINTS

If the pears are very 'wooden', dissolve the sugar (about 1 tbsp per pear) in a little hot water. Use pears for a sponge pudding or crumble.

PLUMS

QUANTITY	COOKING TIME IN MINUTES			
	500w	*600/650w*	*700w*	*800/850w*
225g (8oz)	2½–3½	2–3	1½–2½	1½–2
450g (1lb)	5–6	4–5	3–4	2½–3½

PREPARATION

As for Damsons

WATCHPOINTS

As for Damsons

RHUBARB

QUANTITY	COOKING TIME IN MINUTES			
	500w	*600/650w*	*700w*	*800/850w*
225g (8oz)	5	4	3½	3
450g (1lb)	9½	8	7	5½

PREPARATION

Wash the rhubarb and cut it into short lengths. Add 50g (2oz) or 100g (4oz) caster sugar and the grated zest and juice of a lemon. Toss well. Put the rhubarb in a bowl and cover with pierced clingfilm.

WATCHPOINTS

Shake the rhubarb once or twice during cooking. Serve hot or cold with cream or custard.

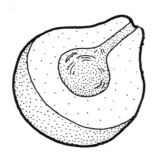

SAUCES

A good sauce can transform an ordinary dish into something special and helps to make foods go further. Microwaving sauces isn't much quicker than cooking by conventional means, but the sauce is smooth and almost failsafe, and there is no dirty saucepan to wash up afterwards.

The most useful sauce for microwaves is basic white, which can be flavoured in many different ways.

FROZEN BASIC SAUCE

Basic microwave sauce can be frozen in boil-in-the-bag packs in 300ml (½pt) quantities. To use, start from frozen for 5 minutes on DEFROST/MED-LOW then cook for 3–5 minutes on FULL/HIGH, shaking the bag from time to time.

HOLLANDAISE AND BEARNAISE SAUCES

Classic Hollandaise and béarnaise sauces can both be made in the microwave and are less likely to curdle than if made by conventional means. Do not freeze these sauces.

GRAVY

The gravy for the Sunday roast can be made in the microwave and kept warm or re-heated as needed. Pour the meat juices away from the joint in the usual way. Make up to 300ml (½pt) with beef or chicken stock or vegetable cooking water. Mix 1 tbsp cornflour in a little water and pour into the gravy mixture. Cook on FULL/HIGH until thickened, stirring every minute.

SAUCE COOKING TIMES

BASIC WHITE

QUANTITY	COOKING TIME IN MINUTES ON FULL			
	500w	*600/650w*	*700w*	*800/850w*
300ml (½pt)	4–5	3½–4	3–3½	2½–3

PREPARATION

Melt 25g (1oz) butter in a jug. Stir in 25g (1oz) plain flour. Gradually stir in 300ml (½pt) milk.

WATCHPOINTS

Stir every minute. Whisk well after cooking.

FLAVOURINGS:

Add any of the following 1 minute before the end of cooking.

Cheese sauce: 75g (3oz) grated cheese, pinch of mustard.

Mushroom sauce: 50g (2oz) sliced sautéed mushrooms.

Onion sauce: 100g (4oz) chopped, sautéed onion.

Parsley sauce: 2 tbsp freshly chopped parsley.

Egg sauce: 1–2 hard-boiled eggs chopped.

White wine sauce: Replace a wine glassful of milk with a wine glassful of dry white wine.

Sweet sauces: Add 25g (1oz) sugar to the milk.

Chocolate sauce: Stir in 2 tbsp cocoa powder dissolved in hot water.

HOLLANDAISE

QUANTITY
Serves 4

COOKING TIME
Cook for 1–1½ minutes on SIMMER/
MEDIUM. Whisk well until thickened and
serve at once.

PREPARATION

Melt 100g (4oz) butter on SIMMER/MEDIUM. Beat in 2 tbsp wine
vinegar and 2 egg yolks.

BEARNAISE

QUANTITY
Serves 4

COOKING TIME
Cook as for Hollandaise sauce

PREPARATION

Cook 1 finely chopped small onion and 1 tbsp fresh choped tarragon
leaves in 2 tbsp wine vinegar for 3–4 minutes on FULL/HIGH. Beat
in 2 egg yolks.

CONVENIENCE FOODS

- Many ready-made foods can be re-heated in the microwave: Pizzas, canned soups, baked beans and spaghetti, ready-prepared frozen meals, fish or other foods frozen in sauce and canned stews. Anything in foil or a can must be removed from the packaging.

- Many frozen meals now have microwave instructions. If the pack does not have instructions, then it is likely that the food inside is not suitable for microwaving.

- Ready-made pies and sausage rolls can be re-heated in the microwave but the pastry turns unpleasantly soggy. This can be rectified by putting under a pre-heated grill briefly.

- Plated meals are a particularly convenient way to provide food in a hurry. Simply freeze the meal on the plate. Meat should have gravy or a sauce to prevent it drying out in the freezer. The meal can be re-heated in the microwave if needed. Plate stacking rings mean that more than one meal can be heated at a time (see p.111).

- Foods frozen in sauce and wrapped in boil-in-the-bag packs re-heat well. Remember to pierce the bag before cooking.

- Chilled, ready-prepared meals must be heated to at least 75°C/170°F right through to the centre and this means cooking at the recommended temperature for the correct time.

MICROWAVE LABELLING

* Reproduced courtesy of the Ministry of Agriculture, Fisheries and Food.

The front of most new domestic microwave ovens now display a label which ties in with new labels on food packs. Matching the information on the food pack with that on the oven will give the heating time needed. The oven label, an example of which is given here, shows three important pieces of information.

the microwave symbol   the power output (watts)

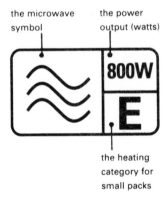

the heating category for small packs

The microwave symbol
The microwave symbol shows that the oven has been labelled in compliance with the new scheme

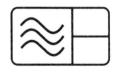

The power output

The figure in this box shows the power output of the oven, in watts, based on an internationally agreed standard (IEC 705).

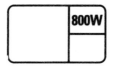

If your oven is rated 600w it will heat food faster than a 500w oven, but not as fast as a 700w or 800/850w oven.

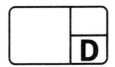

The heating category

In this box, there will be a letter. This is the heating category based on the oven's ability to heat small food packs. Instructions on food packs up to 500g are likely to be given in terms of these letters.

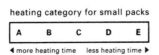

If your oven is category B it will heat up small portions of food faster than category A but not as fast as a category C or D oven.

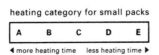

The food pack label

Most packaged food suitable for microwaving will be marked with the microwave symbol and appropriate instructions for heating. Here is an illustration of the type of label used.

≈ **T O   M I C R O W A V E**

For ovens marked with a heating category, select appropriate time(s) for your oven. For other ovens, refer to timings given for oven wattage. When using ovens of different power, heating time must be increased or decreased accordingly. Always check that the food is piping hot before serving.

heating category		oven wattage	
B	D	650W	750W
6	5	5	4
m i n u t e s		m i n u t e s	

Using heating category instructions

In the illustration, information is given for B and D ovens only.

● For C ovens, choose the time midway between B and D, in this case 5½ minutes.

● For A oven, it will be necessary to heat food for a little longer than the time given for B ovens, in this case 6½ minutes.

● For E ovens, use a slightly shorter heating time than that specified for D ovens, in this case 4½ minutes.

After heating, always check that the food if piping hot throughout.

Using oven wattage instructions

In the illustration, information is given for 650w and 750w ovens. For ovens with a wattage lower than 650w, heat for a longer time, for example, a 500w oven will need approximately 6 minutes. For ovens with wattage higher than 750w heat for a slightly shorter time. For example, an 850w oven will need approximately 3 minutes. After heating, always check food is piping hot throughout.

Foodline

If you need further help to understand the instructions on food packs, a free helpline is available through the Food Safety Advisory Centre to offer practical advice.

Freephone: 0800 282 407

CONVENIENCE FOODS RE-HEATING TIMES

Times given are for FULL/HIGH setting unless otherwise stated. Always check food is piping hot right through before serving. Follow microwave labels on packaging where appropriate. Use the following as a guide.

CANNED SAVOURY MINCE OR STEW

QUANTITY

COOKING TIME IN MINUTES

	500w	600/650w	700w	800/850w
one 425g (15oz) can	5–6	4–5	3½–4	3–3½

PREPARATION

Turn into a bowl. Cover with pierced clingfilm.

STANDING TIME

Cover with foil, stand 2 minutes

WATCHPOINTS

Stir once or twice during re-heating. Top with mashed potato and brown under grill to make instant shepherd's pie (no need for standing time then).

FROZEN SHEPHERD'S PIE

FAMILY SIZE

QUANTITY

COOKING TIME IN MINUTES

	500w	600/650w	700w	800/850w
450g (1lb) size	6–7	5–6	4½–5	3½–4

PREPARATION

If in foil, take out and put on a plate. Cover with pierced clingfilm.

DEFROST AND STANDING TIME

6 minutes on DEFROST/MED-LOW then 6 minutes standing before cooking. Cover with foil, stand 3 minutes before serving.

INDIVIDUAL

QUANTITY	COOKING TIME IN MINUTES			
	500w	*600/650w*	*700w*	*800/850w*
1	2–3½	1½–2	1–1½	1

PREPARATION

If in foil, take out and put on a plate. Cover with pierced clingfilm.

DEFROST AND STANDING TIME

4 minutes on DEFROST/MED-LOW then 2 minutes standing before cooking. Cover with foil and stand 2 minutes after cooking.

INDIVIDUAL STEAK AND KIDNEY PUDDING, CANNED

QUANTITY	COOKING TIME IN MINUTES			
	500w	*600/650w*	*700w*	*800/850w*
1	3–4	2½–3	2–2½	1½–2

PREPARATION

Remove from can and turn out on to a plate. Cover with pierced clingfilm.

STANDING TIME

Stand for 2 minutes before serving.

FROZEN LASAGNE

QUANTITY	COOKING TIME IN MINUTES			
	500w	*600/650w*	*700w*	*800/850w*
450g (1lb)	11	9	8	6½

PREPARATION

Turn out if packed in foil. Cover with pierced clingfilm or a dome.

DEFROST AND STANDING TIME

8 minutes on DEFROST/MED-LOW then 6 minutes standing. Stand for 2 minutes after cooking.

WATCHPOINTS

Brown top under grill if wished.

BOIL-IN-THE BAG FROZEN STEW/ CASSEROLE

QUANTITY	COOKING TIME IN MINUTES			
	500w	*600/650w*	*700w*	*800/850w*
one portion	5	4	3½	3

PREPARATION

Pierce bag and stand on a plate.

WATCHPOINTS

Shake bag once or twice during cooking.

BOIL-IN-THE BAG FISH IN SAUCE

QUANTITY	COOKING TIME IN MINUTES			
	500w	*600/650w*	*700w*	*800/850w*
one portion	5	4	3½	3

PREPARATION

Slit bag and place on plate.

STANDING TIME

2 minutes

WATCHPOINTS

Shake once or twice.

CANNED OR CARTON SOUP

QUANTITY	COOKING TIME IN MINUTES			
	500w	*600/650w*	*700w*	*800/850w*
300ml (½pt)	5	4	3½	3

PREPARATION

Turn into two serving bowls or mugs.

WATCHPOINTS

Stir once during cooking.

FROZEN MACARONI CHEESE

QUANTITY	COOKING TIME IN MINUTES			
	500w	*600/650w*	*700w*	*800/850w*
425g (15oz)	7	6	5	4

PREPARATION

Remove from foil packing and place on a plate. Cover with dome.

DEFROST AND STANDING TIME

8 minutes on DEFROST/MED-LOW then 6 minutes standing before cooking. Stir before cooking. Stand 2 minutes after cooking.

WATCHPOINTS

Stir once or twice during cooking.

CANNED PASTA

QUANTITY	COOKING TIME IN MINUTES			
	500w	*600/650w*	*700w*	*800/850w*
Large can	5	4	3½	3

PREPARATION

Turn into a bowl or serving dish. Cover with pierced clingfilm. Or prepare on toast as for baked beans below.

WATCHPOINTS

Stir once or twice during cooking.

BAKED BEANS

QUANTITY	COOKING TIME IN MINUTES			
	500w	*600/650w*	*700w*	*800/850w*
220G (7¼oz	2	1½	1¼	1
425g (15½oz)	5	4	3½	3

PREPARATION

Turn into a bowl or serving dish. Cover with pierced clingfilm. Or make toast conventionally. Put on plate, add beans, cook as for 220g (7¼oz) quantity above.

WATCHPOINTS

Stir once or twice during cooking (if cooking in a bowl).

FROZEN PLATED MEAL

QUANTITY	COOKING TIME IN MINUTES			
	500w	*600/650w*	*700w*	*800/850w*
1 (150g/5oz meat in gravy, mashed potatoes, 2 veg)	5	4	3½	3

PREPARATION

Cook the meal in its wrapping.

DEFROST AND STANDING TIME

5 minutes on DEFROST/MED-LOW then 2 minutes standing before cooking.

WATCHPOINTS

Always arrange plated meals with densest, thickest foods towards the outside. To reheat non-frozen plated meals, use cooking times above.

OVEN CHIPS

QUANTITY	COOKING TIME IN MINUTES			
	500w	*600/650w*	*700w*	*800/850w*
225g (8oz)	4	3½	3	2½

PREPARATION

Oven chips can only be microwaved in a browning dish. Pre-heat the dish on FULL/HIGH for 5 minutes or according to manufacturer's instructions.

WATCHPOINTS

Stir the chips once or twice during cooking.

CUP OF COFFEE/TEA

QUANTITY	COOKING TIME IN MINUTES			
	500w	*600/650w*	*700w*	*800/850w*
1 cup/mug (200ml/⅓pt)	2½	2	1½–2	1–1½

PREPARATION

Make sure cup is microwave safe.

WATCHPOINTS

Stir before drinking.

EGGS

A microwave will produce deliciously fluffy scrambled eggs. Other egg dishes can be cooked with equal success. Baked and poached eggs are both very good.

• It is essential that egg yolks are pierced for any dish where the yolk remains whole. Egg yolk is covered by a transparent membrane. If this isn't pierced, the yolk will explode during microwaving. Piercing this membrane does not mean that the egg yolk will run during cooking. A sharp prod from a cocktail stick is all that is needed.

• Fried eggs can be cooked but it isn't really worth the effort. A frying pan is more effective.

• Don't try and boil eggs in their shell – they'll explode!

POACHED EGGS

For all power outputs.

1. Put about 2.5cm (1in) boiling water in each microwave-safe ramekin dish.

2. Break one egg into each ramekin (four is the maximum number which will microwave well) and pierce the yolks.
3. Microwave the eggs on FULL/HIGH for 30 seconds per egg. Remove from the microwave as soon as the egg white is set. The egg will continue to cook for a few seconds after removal.

BAKED EGGS

For all power outputs. Melt a knob of butter in the base of microwave-safe ramekin dishes. (30 seconds on FULL/HIGH.) Break an egg into each ramekin, pierce yolks, top with 1 tsp double cream and cook for 15 seconds per egg on FULL/HIGH. Stand for 1 minute then cook the eggs for a further 15 seconds on FULL/HIGH.

SCRAMBLED EGGS

Allow two eggs per person. Eight is the maximum which will scramble well in the microwave. Beat the eggs in a jug with 1–2 tbsp milk per egg. Add a knob of butter and season to taste.

Per egg: Cook on FULL/HIGH for 1¼ minutes (*500w*). 1 minute (*600/650w*), ¾ minute (*700w*), ½–¾ minute (*800/850w*).

RICE, PASTA AND PULSES

Although rice, pasta and pulses don't cook much faster in the microwave than they do by conventional means, the results are good. Rice grains won't stick together, pasta is tender but has 'bite' and, best of all, the kitchen remains free of steam.

Rice, pasta and pulses are all cooked in boiling water, so the container must be big.

RICE

Long-grain and easy-cook long-grain rice are cooked in the microwave using salted water. A failsafe method is to use a lot of water and drain the rice after cooking. Brown rice can also be cooked in this way.

Frozen rice can be defrosted and re-heated in one simply operation. Simply turn the rice into a container, cover, and stir as it thaws. Risottos, kedgeree and other rice-based dishes can be defrosted and re-heated in the same way.

PASTA

Don't cook more than 450g (1lb) pasta in the microwave, as it is difficult to get a large enough microwave container for this amount.

Frozen plain pasta (without sauce) can be defrosted and re-heated in the same way as rice.

Fresh pasta will take literally one or two minutes to cook. Check frequently for doneness.

PULSES

Pulses except red lentils must be soaked for 8–12 hours before microwaving. The time advantage is not very great, as most pulses take over an hour to cook in the microwave, so you may prefer to use conventional means. If you do cook pulses in the microwave, don't add salt before cooking as it toughens the skins. Use plenty of boiling water and cook on full power. Test after 45 minutes then continue cooking in 5 minute bursts. Allow to stand 5 minutes after cooking, covered in foil.

COUSCOUS AND BULGAR

Couscous should be cooked in water for about 4 minutes.

Bulgar should be cooked for 3 minutes, then add boiling water and cook for a further 5 minutes, stirring occasionally.

RICE, PASTA AND PULSES COOKING TIMES

Times given are for FULL/HIGH setting.

MACARONI

QUANTITY	COOKING TIME IN MINUTES			
	500w	*600/650w*	*700w*	*800/850w*
225g (8oz)	12	10	8½	7

PREPARATION

Add 550ml (1pt) boiling salted water and 1 tsp oil.

STANDING TIME

5 minutes covered in foil.

WATCHPOINTS

For quick-cook macaroni reduce cooking time by 1–2 minutes.

NOODLES/TAGLIATELLE

QUANTITY	COOKING TIME IN MINUTES			
	500w	*600/650w*	*700w*	*800/850w*
225g (8oz)	7–9½	6–8	5–7	4–5½

PREPARATION

Add 600ml (1pt) boiling salted water and 1 tsp oil.

STANDING TIME

5 minutes.

WATCHPOINTS

Stir half way through cooking.

RICE

BROWN

QUANTITY	COOKING TIME IN MINUTES			
	500w	*600/650w*	*700w*	*800/850w*
225g (8oz)	32½	27	23	19

PREPARATION

Add 600ml (1pt) boiling salted water. Cover.

STANDING TIME

5 minutes.

WATCHPOINTS

Stir half way through cooking.

LONG GRAIN

QUANTITY	COOKING TIME IN MINUTES			
	500w	*600/650w*	*700w*	*800/850w*
225g (8oz)	18	15	13	10½

PREPARATION

As for Brown rice.

STANDING TIME

5 minutes.

WATCHPOINTS

Stir half way through cooking.

SPAGHETTI

QUANTITY	COOKING TIME IN MINUTES			
	500w	*600/650w*	*700w*	*800/850w*
225g (8oz)	15½	13	11	9

PREPARATION

Break in half. Add 600ml (1pt) boiling salted water and 1 tsp oil.

STANDING TIME

5 minutes.

WATCHPOINTS

Stir halfway through cooking.

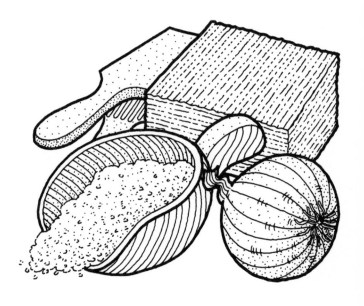

BAKING AND DESSERTS

Because baking is a cooking method which needs dry heat, cakes, biscuits, and breads are not ideally suited to microwave cooking. But it does have its uses in this area. It can be used to reduce the proving time needed for home-baked bread, to make light, delicious sponge puddings, instant cakes (useful when unexpected guests arrive for tea), and to thaw cheesecakes, gâteaux and frozen desserts.

Your microwave will help you to make perfect baked custards, milk puddings and traditional suet favourites. It can also be used to melt the gelatine needed for setting cold puddings, to cook fruit for purée-based desserts (see Fruit chapter), to melt chocolate and to make sweet sauces (see Sauces chapter).

BREAD

The dough for any bread recipe can be proved in the microwave.

1. Mix the dough and knead it in the usual way.

2. Cover the dough with clingfilm before proving in the microwave: start the proving with 10 minutes at the lowest setting on your microwave (10 percent of full power).

3. Give 10 minutes rest then continue alternating 10 minutes microwaving with 10 minutes resting until the dough has doubled in size. (An alternative method is to give 15 seconds at FULL/HIGH, then 8 minutes rest. This is quicker but needs great care as too much heat can start the dough cooking at the edges. This will kill the yeast and the end result will be a loaf with the texture of a brick.

4. After rising, the dough is kneaded again (this part of the process is called knocking back), shaped and put into the container which will be used for cooking.

5. If the bread needs a second proving, this must be done conventionally if the loaf is to be cooked in a normal oven.

Bread can be cooked in the microwave but doesn't brown. Also the crust will be soft, and the bread tends to overcook at the ends. It will stale quickly too.

Our chart gives timings for a 450g (1lb) brown or white loaf.

CAKES

Sponge mixtures cook quickly in the microwave, and although the cake won't brown, this doesn't matter if it contains naturally brown colour, such as coffee or chocolate, or if it is to be iced. Microwaved sponge mixtures are light and taste home-baked, but will stale quickly.

Microwave cakes can be baked in any microwave-safe dish, or in special microwave bakeware, available from microwave specialists such as Lakeland Plastics, Alexandra Buildings, Station Road, Windermere, Cumbria.

Traditional fruit cakes do not work well in a microwave, as the outside tends to dry out before the centre is cooked.

GOLDEN RULES FOR BAKING CAKES

• Microwave sponge cakes rise quickly, so allow plenty of headspace in the container.

• Remove the cake from the microwave while it is still slightly moist. Cooking continues for a short time after the cake has been removed from the oven.

• When cooked, though still with 'wet spots' the cake will have shrunk from the edge of the container or will pull away easily.

• Allow the cake to cool for 15–20 minutes before turning out.

• Microwave scones are possible, but have a poor flavour. It is better to make scones in the conventional oven, freeze them, then thaw/re-heat in the microwave.

• Use butter rather than margarine for better colour.

• Use light brown sugar and substitute either the whole amount or half the amount of white flour with wholemeal flour.

• Make sure that sugar is not lumpy as this can result in burned patches through the cake.

• Don't flour cake pans as flour can produce a coating on the cake.

- For cakes such as gingerbread that are made by the melting method, melt the fat and sugar in a heatproof bowl in the microwave.

- If syrup or honey has crystallised, microwave on HIGH for 1–2 minutes until melted. Similarly, hardened sugar, marzipan or fondant icing can be softened in the microwave.

PUDDINGS

- **Milk puddings, custards, sponge puddings and suet mixtures** are all successful in the microwave, especially suet and sponge puddings.

- To **melt chocolate**, break the chocolate into pieces and microwave on 70 percent power, stirring from time to time.

- **Gelatine** for set mixtures can be dissolved in the microwave. Sprinkle the gelatine on to liquid, as instructed in the recipe you are using. Put the bowl in the microwave and cook on FULL/HIGH for 30–55 seconds until the gelatine has melted.

- **Rice, semolina, tapioca and sago** can all be cooked in the microwave. The results are rich and creamy, and take only a fraction of the time needed for conventional cooking.

- Use the microwave to make **Christmas pudding** – it takes about 20 minutes to make and only about 2 minutes to reheat. Ingredients such as treacle, dark brown sugar and wholemeal flour create colour and flavour. To flame the pudding, warm brandy first in a cup in the microwave before pouring over the pudding and setting it alight.

- **Caramel** can be safely and easily made in a microwave. Crème caramel is very much quicker to make in a microwave.

- **Meringues** work well in a microwave providing that you use the exact amount of sugar and egg whites that are specified in the recipe. The meringue is white and perfectly dried out. Meringue can also be used to top a fruit pudding, if there is not too much liquid in the fruit which would cause the meringue to become soggy.

DEFROSTING CAKES, BREADS AND PUDDINGS

The microwave is invaluable for defrosting bread and plain cakes without icing, for cooking sponge puddings from frozen and for speeding the thawing of gâteaux and cream puddings.

CAKES

• Thaw plain cakes in their wrapping.

• Don't completely thaw iced or cream cakes as the topping and filling will melt. But start thawing them in the microwave, as shown in the chart.

BREAD

Baked bread will keep in the freezer for up to four months and, once thawed, will taste as good as when it was freshly made.

• Thaw wrapped loaves in their bag, but make sure that the tie at the end of the bag does not have a metal core.

• Rolls and croissants should be thawed unwrapped. Stand them on a piece of absorbent kitchen paper with another piece of paper over the top to absorb moisture.

• You can also 'freshen' slightly stale bread by wrapping it in a clean dish cloth and warming it on DEFROST/MED-LOW for 15–30 seconds. But don't overdo it and eat immediately.

MOUSSES AND SET PUDDINGS

Like cream cakes, mousses cannot be completely thawed in the microwave, but natural thawing can be speeded up with a burst of microwave energy.

PASTRY DISHES

• Don't microwave thaw pies as it is easy to start the pastry cooking. Most frozen pies can be cooked in the conventional oven from frozen.

• But you can thaw raw, frozen pastry, either home-made or bought, in the microwave but don't be tempted to cut corners by reducing the standing time and increasing microwaving since the fat in the pastry will start to melt.

BREAD AND CAKES THAWING TIMES

Thaw bread and cakes on DEFROST/MED-LOW. There is no need to adjust times for this as there is very little difference between microwaves at this level.

BREAD

WHITE/BROWN

QUANTITY   **DEFROST TIME**
Large sliced loaf   6–7 minutes

WATCHPOINTS

Leave wrapped, but open end of bag. Stand 10–15 minutes to allow heat to spread through loaf.

WHITE/BROWN

QUANTITY   **DEFROST TIME**
Small sliced loaf   3–4 minutes

WATCHPOINTS

As above, but stand 5–10 minutes.

WHITE/BROWN

QUANTITY   **DEFROST TIME**
1 medium slice   30 seconds

WATCHPOINTS

Check halfway as a slice hardens quickly.

WHITE/BROWN

QUANTITY   **DEFROST TIME**
Small unsliced loaf or
   Vienna   4–5 minutes

WATCHPOINTS

Unwrap and place on absorbent kitchen paper. Cover loosely with kitchen paper. Stand for 5–10 minutes.

WHITE/BROWN

QUANTITY   **DEFROST TIME**
Large unsliced loaf   7–8 minutes

WATCHPOINTS

Unwrap and place on absorbent kitchen paper. Cover with another sheet of kitchen paper. Stand for 10–15 minutes.

BREAD ROLLS

QUANTITY   **DEFROST TIME**
2   1 minute
4   2 minutes

WATCHPOINTS

Place on absorbent kitchen paper and cover with another sheet of kitchen paper. Stand 2 rolls for 2 minutes, 4 rolls for 3 minutes.

FRUIT BREAD BUNS

QUANTITY   **DEFROST TIME**
2   1 minute
4   2 minutes

WATCHPOINTS

Place on absorbent kitchen paper and cover with another sheet of kitchen paper. Stand for 5–8 minutes.

CHEESECAKE

QUANTITY   **DEFROST TIME**
one 15cm (6in)
  cheesecake   3 minutes

WATCHPOINTS

Place on absorbent kitchen paper. Stand for 25 minutes. Long standing is essential to complete thawing.

CROISSANTS

QUANTITY
2
4

DEFROST TIME
1 minute
2 minutes

WATCHPOINTS

Place on absorbent kitchen paper and cover with another sheet of kitchen paper. Stand for 2 minutes. Give another 30 seconds–1 minute on FULL for hot croissants. Note that the pastry will not be crisp.

DOUGHNUTS

CREAM DOUGHNUTS

QUANTITY
2
4

DEFROST TIME
45 seconds
1½ minutes

WATCHPOINTS

Place uncovered on absorbent kitchen paper. Check halfway through. Remove if cream has started melting and allow longer standing. Stand for 5 minutes, then pop into the fridge for a couple of minutes to chill the cream.

JAM DOUGHNUTS

QUANTITY
2
4

DEFROST TIME
1½ minutes
2½ minutes

WATCHPOINTS

Place on a plate covered with absorbent kitchen paper. Check halfway through. Stand for 2 minutes for two, 5 minutes for four.
WARNING: The jam inside will be very hot.

ECLAIRS

QUANTITY
2
4

DEFROST TIME
15 seconds
1 minute

WATCHPOINTS

Place on absorbent kitchen paper. Stand for 10 minutes. Check cream and chocolate for signs of melting.

CREAM GATEAUX

QUANTITY
one 15cm (6in) gâteau
one 20cm (8in) gâteau

DEFROST TIME
3 minutes
5 minutes

WATCHPOINTS

Place gâteau on absorbent kitchen paper. Stand for 1 hour for 15cm (6in), 2 hours for 20cm (8in). Do not be tempted to increase the microwaving time as the cream will melt.

SAFETY NOTES

- Always read the manufacturer's instructions before use.

- Check that door seals are clean and grease-free.

- Never use abrasive cleaners in the microwave.

- Have the microwave regularly serviced.

- Don't leave a microwave unattended when in use.

- Fatty and sugary foods can overheat and burn or even catch fire. Be careful with cooking times and never leave the foods unattended.

- Stir liquids before and during cooking.

- Be aware that cups can become very hot after heating in a microwave so check before drinking from them.

- Use containers large enough to contain the food and to allow expansion so that the food does not bubble over the top.

- Do not use sealed containers as these could burst with the build up of steam.

- Always use oven gloves to protect your hands when removing hot containers from the microwave.

GENERAL
MICROWAVE TIPS

- To blanch almonds, cover with boiling water and heat in the microwave for 1 minute until almost boiling. Remove and leave to stand for a few minutes, then the skins will slip off easily.

- Brown breadcrumbs on FULL for about 5 minutes, tossing occasionally.

- Melt or soften butter in about 30 seconds.

- Grate rather than slice cheese so that it melts evenly.

- To refresh coffee beans, put 2 tablespoons in the microwave in a bowl lined with kitchen paper. Place a cup of water in the oven and microwave for 30 seconds.

- To plump up dried fruits, cover with water and cook on FULL for 4 minutes until soft and plump, then drain.

- Soften ice cream on LOW or DEFROST for about 1 minute before serving.

- Melt jam for about 30 seconds for glazing pies and cakes.

- To toast nuts, arrange in a single layer on a tray with a knob of butter and cook for 2 minutes until just golden, shaking frequently.

- Prepare poppadoms in the microwave for about 30 seconds for the first and an additional 10 seconds for each extra poppadom.

- Mix porridge and water in a bowl and microwave on FULL for about 3 minutes, stirring twice. Leave to stand for 1 minute before stirring and serving.

- To sterilise jars for preserves, half-fill with water and heat until boiling, then boil for 1 minute. Remove carefully and drain. Do not use for babies' bottles or teats.